"These books will make super resources for Sunday school classes, for thoughtful church leaders, and indeed for all Christians who want to take their faith, and its ecumenical history, seriously."

Carl R. Trueman, Westminster Theological Seminary

"Faithful wisdom through the centuries needs to be explored for our own engagement with Scripture today.... You won't regret the journey."

Michael Horton, author, *Core Christianity*

KNOW
HOW WE GOT
OUR BIBLE

Other Books in the Know Series

KNOW
HOW WE GOT OUR BIBLE

RYAN M. REEVES AND CHARLES E. HILL

JUSTIN S. HOLCOMB, SERIES EDITOR

ZONDERVAN

Know How We Got Our Bible

Copyright © 2018 by Ryan M. Reeves and Charles E. Hill

This title is also available as a Zondervan ebook.

This title is also available as a Zondervan audio book.

Requests for information should be addressed to:

Zondervan, 3900 Sparks Dr. SE, Grand Rapids, Michigan 49546

ISBN 978-0-310-53720-5

Cover design: Gearbox
Interior design: Greg Johnson / Textbook Perfect

Printed in the United States of America

18 19 20 21 22 /DHV/ 10 9 8 7 6 5 4 3 2 1

*We dedicate this book to the loyal teachers
who first taught us our Bibles.*

CONTENTS

FOREWORD

How did we get the Bible? When was the Bible written? How can we trust the Bible? How did the Word of God go from God's mind to people in an ancient Near Eastern culture to the Christians of the first century to your hands and ears?

How We Got Our Bible answers these questions.

This book began in 1996 in CR2 (classroom two) of Reformed Theological Seminary in Orlando, when I took a course by Dr. Charles Hill in which he taught about canonization. The story of the writing, transmission, copying, and canonization of Holy Scripture fascinated me and my friend Ryan Reeves. Ryan had a similar experience with Dr. Hill in 2002, and the foundation for the book was laid.

The Bible we have in our hands, on our phones, and recorded so you can listen to it comes to us through a long series of faithful copying and translation throughout the centuries.

We also have discovered older manuscripts that we thought were lost, earlier versions of certain texts, like the Greek Bible. But in general, what we have is a series of faithful transmission.

Translations, in some ways, are just copies of the existing Bible. The words are translated, they're copied over, and they're reworked and checked and rechecked against the originals. You end up with a copy of the Bible. In English too we have a number of translations to choose from today, and those stories need to be told.

To tell the longer and more compelling version of the story, with all the twists and turns of history, I invited the two best people

I could think of: Charles Hill and Ryan Reeves. Charles is still professor of New Testament and early Christianity at Reformed Theological Seminary. He continued to research the material that fascinated me (in 1996) and Ryan (in 2002) and published two books on the topic (*Who Chose the Gospels? Probing the Great Gospel Conspiracy* and *The Early Text of the New Testament* [with Michael J. Kruger]). Ryan ended up earning a doctorate in church history after seminary and is a professor at Gordon-Conwell Theological Seminary. He is one of the best teachers I know. One sign of brilliance is to be able to take high-level concepts and information and make easy to understand and interesting. Ryan is masterful at this. Together, Charles and Ryan make great tour guides through the story of how the manuscripts of sacred texts from thousands of years ago made it to us.

This story is not only fascinating but important. The Bible is the most significant and influential book in the world because it is the Word of God.[1] The Bible tells us who God is and who we are. Ultimately the Bible is about how God created and is redeeming the world through Jesus Christ. The Old Testament begins with the creation of the world and develops the story of God's redemptive plan all the way through the destruction of Jerusalem in 586 BC and into the Babylonian exile. There are about four-hundred years between the Old and New Testaments, and then this story of redemption continues with the incarnation, ministry, death, resurrection, and ascension of Jesus Christ, the Son of God, followed by the expansion of the kingdom of God until Jesus Christ returns and establishes the new heavens and new earth.

God is active. He created all things, delivered his people from bondage in Egypt, and took on a human nature to live and die and rise again. Not only does God act in history, but he also interprets his actions by inspiring Holy Scripture. God inspires Genesis to interpret his creative actions. God gives Exodus to interpret his action of freeing his people from bondage. God provides the New Testament to interpret the life, death, resurrection, and ascension of Jesus Christ and what it means for him to bring the kingdom of God. The divine author, the Holy Spirit, inspired the human authors of the Bible to bear witness to the drama of redemption in both the history of Israel and the life, death, and resurrection of Jesus Christ. The Bible is a series of divinely inspired interpretations of the acts of God.

The Bible therefore "contains all things necessary to salvation"[2] and is a primary way God leads us: "Your word is a lamp for my feet, a light on my path" (Psalm 119:105). This is why knowing how we got our Bible is story that is both interesting and vital.

Justin S. Holcomb

GLOSSARY

Apocrypha: The books written between the Old and New Testament periods; important documents in Jewish history. They are considered part of the Bible for Catholics and Orthodox Christians, but are not in Protestant Bibles. They should not be confused with apocryphal books, which are often heretical.

Authorized Version: The Bible compiled under the reign of King James of England (1566–1625), which is popularly known in North America as the "King James Bible." In fact, it was not given royal approval or authorization, so both names are technically inaccurate.

canon: The canon is the set number of books or texts that are considered Scripture and make up the books of the Bible. The word originally meant in Greek a "rule" or "measure."

Dead Sea Scrolls: See Qumran.

deuterocanonical: Books that may be included in the Bible but (for various reasons) are given lower status, or are seen as supplementary to other biblical books. For example, Lutheranism sees the Apocrypha as deuterocanonical.

Diaspora: The Jewish migration around the known world, beginning before the birth of Christ but increasing dramatically after the destruction of Jerusalem in AD 70.

dynamic equivalence: A method of translating the Bible in a thought-for-thought style, not a word-for-word style.

Erasmus: A humanist scholar and linguist during the Reformation who compiled a landmark edition of the Greek New Testament.

Greek New Testament: For convenience, we often say *the* Greek New Testament, but strictly speaking there is no single copy of the Greek New Testament. We have thousands of copies and fragments of copies that, together, allow us to reconstruct the original Greek text of the New Testament books.

Gutenberg press: The first printing press to use movable type or letters on a grid that could be easily rearranged. It was not the first printing press, but a revolution in printing technology.

Hebrew Bible: See Jewish canon.

Jerome: Translator of the Vulgate. See Vulgate.

Jewish canon: Those books acknowledged as inspired by God and authoritative by the Israelites, as well as the arrangement of the books into the TaNaK. It can also be called the "Hebrew Bible."

Ketuvim: See TaNaK.

King James Bible: See Authorized Version.

Leningrad Codex: The oldest complete copy of the Hebrew Bible, named for a city in Russia (Leningrad, now Saint Petersburg) where it is stored.

LXX: A shorthand way of referring to the Septuagint (i.e., the Greek translation of the Old Testament).

manuscript: Any text written by hand. Not a printed text.

Marcion: An early opponent of the canon of the Bible. He wanted all of the Old Testament and most of the New Testament removed in order to purge Christian theology of its Jewish foundation.

Masoretes: Rabbinical scholars who transcribed Hebrew copies of the Old Testament in the Middle Ages. They added vowel pointing to make copying and reading the text easier.

Nevi'im: See TaNaK.

Octateuch: A practice in the Middle Ages of binding the first eight ("octa-") books of the Bible into one volume. The practice was common before technology allowed printers to make a single-volume Bible.

papyrus: An ancient writing material made from the papyrus plant. It is extremely vulnerable in wet conditions and prone to decay from age, which is why many papyri are lost today and remains are mostly fragments.

parchment: A writing material made from animal skin, used mostly in the Middle Ages. Distinguished from papyrus or paper.

Pentateuch: The first five ("penta-") books of the Bible.

Qumran: A discovery in the 1940s of the remains of an ancient Jewish community. Important for its stockpile of Old Testament and extracanonical texts. The texts discovered are often called the Dead Sea Scrolls.

Septuagint: The Greek translation of the Old Testament that was completed before the birth of Christ. In reality, there were several translations of the Old Testament into Greek.

TaNaK: Another way to describe the Jewish arrangement of the Old Testament. The Israelites divided the Old Testament books into the Law (Torah), the Prophets (Nevi'im), and the Writings (Ketuvim)—so the first letter of each section is used to create the word *TaNaK*.

textual criticism: The study of existing copies of the Bible to determine, as closely as possible, the original form of each biblical book. An important field of study since we do not have the original autographs of the biblical text.

Torah: A Hebrew name for "Law," used as a shorthand reference to the first five books of the Old Testament.

Tyndale, William: An early English Protestant who was the first after Wycliffe to attempt to translate the Bible into English. He was executed before he could complete the Old Testament.

Vulgate: A Bible translation into Latin done by Jerome in the fourth century. The word *vulgar* (borrowed from Latin) meant simply something that was "common"—hence the Vulgate was the Bible in the common Latin language. It became the exclusive Bible of the West in the Middle Ages and remains the authorized translation for the Roman Catholic Church today.

word-for-word translation: A method of translating the Bible that seeks to keep phrases and word order strictly parallel to the original language. Sometimes called a "literal translation," it is best understood as a method that focuses on achieving a parallel order.

Wycliffe, John: A medieval scholar and statesman from the fourteenth century who was the first to oversee the translation of the entire Bible into English. An opponent of the Catholic Church, he was condemned for his views on the Lord's Supper.

CHAPTER 1

WHO'S ON FIRST

Abbott and Costello are remembered for their comedy routine *"Who's on First?"* The duo first performed the sketch in the 1930s—and it has been a hit with fans ever since.

In the sketch, Abbott plays it straight, and Costello is the clown. The two set up the punch line by pretending that Costello is joining a baseball team. Abbott wants to help him fit in, so he offers to share the nicknames of each of his new teammates. Costello agrees, and Abbott begins to list them rapid-fire. Costello immediately stops the conversation, since he is having trouble following. Abbott continues, but repeats the same names over and over, and Costello by the end has a meltdown.

The confusion is because the nicknames Abbott gives are nonsense. The first baseman is *Who*, the second baseman is *What*, the third baseman is *I Don't Know*. Costello wants answers, but Abbott seems to be refusing to answer his questions:

Costello: What's the guy's name?

Abbott: I told you his name.

Costello: Okay, who's on second base?

Abbott: No, Who's on first base.

Costello: But I don't know the second baseman.

Abbott: Well, I Don't Know's on third.

Costello: What do you mean?!![1]

It is one of the funniest sketches in history. In fact, *Time* magazine named it the best comedy routine of the twentieth century.[2] It is even celebrated in the Baseball Hall of Fame and Museum, which placed a recording of the sketch on display in Cooperstown.

Who's on first, What's on second, I Don't Know's on third.

Costello, of course, is asking the *wrong* question. He is approaching the information without learning Abbott's jargon. If he knew the basics—or at least knew better questions to ask—he could carry on a conversation. The audience sees the humor, of course, because they know that Costello should *rephrase* the question. Ask *which* person is on second, *which* player is on first. Better still, ask Abbott to write down the names—then Costello might realize the problem. Instead, he continues with the same logic, asking the same questions, only now he thinks Abbott is irrational.

Not a few have felt the same way when studying their Bibles. We have all sat in Sunday school classes, or read a study guide to the Bible, and found ourselves lost. Plenty of jargon, not enough explanation. Christians, of course, want to know the Bible, but it can be intimidating if we feel behind on the basics. Where do we begin? Do we learn the book chronologically or shuffle around learning things as they come up? Is there anything I need to know *before* reading my Bible?[3]

Those who feel this way are not alone. For instance, we both work in theological education. We teach at seminaries. The purpose of a seminary is to train pastors, missionaries, church leaders, and people from all walks of life. One of us teaches New Testament, the other church history and theology. But we both share a goal to help students know the Word of God.

Even seminary students occasionally admit they wish they knew more of the basics. For some, classes can feel overwhelming, even if the student is bright, capable, and hardworking. Some end up like Costello without the grammar to form the correct questions. If this is true for those studying in seminary, it certainly can be true for most Christians.

Who's on first, What's on second, I Don't Know's on third.

This is normal for every disciple—the desire to know more about God, to know his Word. But for some of us, the experience can be frustrating. For example, Ryan regularly tells the story of his earliest attempt to read the Bible. He was a new Christian, and so he asked his mother which Gospel had the story of Jesus's death and resurrection. He assumed the Gospels worked like chapters—each one telling the next part of the story. His mother told him the story is in all four Gospels, since each is written highlighting different facets of Jesus's life. Ryan was surprised by this. But now that he knew something about the Bible, he began to ask the right questions: Why would the Bible need to repeat itself? Is one Gospel better than the others? Can we harmonize all of the Gospels into one complete timeline?

Who's on first, What's on second, I Don't Know's on third.

Learning the Bible

The goal of this book is to provide a starting point for those eager to read the Bible. We do not intend this book only for advanced students. The book is for all Christians who need a place to start learning the Bible.

In fact, the first inspiration for this book came during Sunday school. Each week, friends and family arrived with their Bibles—typically a single leather-bound volume. Everyone loved to learn about the Bible, but they did not all have the same version: some liked the ESV (English Standard Version), others the NIV (New International Version), still others the NKJV (New King James Version). It was surprising to see everyone united when we had different Bibles. Another friend once asked why she has so many versions of the Bible on her shelf and where did they all come from? These Bibles need an explanation.

The question for this book is simple—how did a series of ancient texts, written mostly on papyrus in two old languages, get into our hands? How did we get the Bible in *this* format with *these* translations?

The fact is, the Bibles we own are very unlike those in the early church. Not the texts themselves—which have been well preserved—but the *book* we are holding. The shape of it, the size of it, even the arrangement of the books: these are different from what the Israelites and early Christians held in their hands. They held Bibles that were costly to make, in the time spent copying the text and in the materials used. Our Bibles can be expensive, but we also can find an affordable Bible without any difficulty. In fact, most Christians over the centuries never had personal Bibles. Most were illiterate and only heard the Word during worship.

If you wonder about different translations of your favorite verse, you can easily find a way to place several English translations side by side. Just a generation ago, you would have needed access to a library to do this. Medieval Christians, by comparison, had the Latin Vulgate, and most Christians after AD 900 could not understand the langauge. The medieval Bible was the possession of the church, not lay Christians. So modern Christians have the privilege of owning a Bible that very few Christians in history have enjoyed. Each version we own is the product of a team of scholars and pastors who used their gifts to translate the Bible into our native language. Some of that story needs to be told in order for us to realize how we got our Bibles.

Perhaps the most important change in our lifetime is our *access* to the Bible. Some of us have no *physical* copy of the Bible, preferring an app or an online version. Most of us have several physical Bibles and at least one Bible app—and we use them all.

This is illustrated in the success of Daily Audio Bible—a free resource created by Brian Hardin. He simply reads the Bible each morning. No commentary, no sermon; just the Bible read for any who want to listen. And people are listening. As of 2010, Brian's podcast has been downloaded 40 million times.

But in each of these cases, it is still our Bible, even if we read it and hear it in ways unimaginable to earlier Christians.

Perhaps another analogy will help. An Anglo-Saxon riddle asks the following:

> Who am I? First I was killed by an enemy, soaked in water and dried in the sun, where I lost all my hair. After that, I was stretched out and scraped with a knife blade . . . folded, and a bird's feather traveled over my surface. . . . Finally I was bound and covered with skin, gilded, and beautifully decorated.[4]

The answer, of course, is a Bible. The clues reveal how animal skins were obtained, dried, and scraped until they were smooth. The feather is a quill, dipped in ink, and the rest is the decoration of the text—all of which combined to make a style of Bible common in the Middle Ages. But this is not how we would have created the same riddle. In fact, our riddles would be equally strange to the Anglo-Saxons:

Who am I? First, I was felled by an axe, pulped in hot water, and pressed until I was as thin as a whisker. I was left in a hot room to dry. Next, I was pressed with inky steel (some of the letters in red) and wrapped in leather. Though I am nothing like I was, I will be precious to someone.

And now that we are in the twenty-first century, we can go further:

I am a series of zeros and ones, and I am dead without batteries. I speak in Swift, but you cannot speak to me. Tap your finger, and I will tell you anything. When I am awake, I emit a blue light that triggers insomnia. You wish your children would put me down at the dinner table.

Different Bibles, but the same Word of God. This can raise hard questions, but we first need to understand the basics. One place to begin is to learn how we got our Bible.

Basic Questions and Terms

Before we push off on our journey, it would be helpful to know some of the road ahead. In our experience, there are two questions that Christians often ask about the Bible: (1) Are all Bible translations the same? and (2) Is the text of the Bible trustworthy?

To begin, how do we evaluate the various translations of the Bible? If you have studied a foreign language, you know the problem. It is easy enough to learn how to ask for the restroom or to order a meal, but it is another thing to translate poetry. If you worked on the translation of a legal document or new legislation, clearly the stakes would be high. For the sake of the reader, you would need to make sure the original meaning was clear.

When translating any text, there are ultimately two methods. Either you translate each word as closely as possible to the original, using footnotes, perhaps, if there are tricky parts. The second option is you take the original meaning—including the unique phrases and idioms in that language—and draft a translation closer to how it would be expressed in the target language, even if that means ignoring the precise wording of the original document.

In Bible translation, the first method is known as a *word-for-word* method, the second as a *dynamic-equivalent* method. Most people are familiar with the word-for-word method, and some Bible translations make it clear in their advertising that the translation team used it. At times, this method is called a *literal* translation.

In the dynamic equivalent method, translators work to draft a Bible in good English (or another target language), seeking to avoid wooden or confusing wording. The focus is on ensuring the reader can truly understand the text. Essentially, the aim is to provide *parallel ideas*, not strictly *parallel words*.

For works of literature, the most common tactic used was *dynamic equivalence*. If the original words of Dante in *The Divine Comedy* have a beauty in their rhyming, then it makes sense to find an equally pleasant rhyming pattern in a new translation. If you want a copy of Homer's *Iliad* today, you will find at least three main English translations, the most famous done by the poet John Keats. When translating poetry, it is best to hire a poet.

The challenge in Bible translation is that the *words* themselves—the biblical text in Hebrew and Greek—are not just poetry but the inspired Word of God. A great deal of care is taken to ensure that the words are communicated accurately in the translation. It is also necessary to ensure that readers can easily understand the translation.

Still, the two approaches are closer than it may seem. Word-for-word Bible translation sometimes must use dynamic equivalent translation, and dynamic equivalent Bibles often strive for word-for-word translation.

For example, Mark 1:2 quotes from Malachi that John the Baptist will prepare the way for Jesus. The literal phrase in the Greek is that he will "go before your face," which is not an expression we use in English.[5] One can imagine a child attempting to read this literally! The phrase simply means "go before," so nearly all English translations—even translations that strive to be word for word—render this phrase in more readable English.[6] This is often necessary when translating Hebrew too, which has idioms that are impossible to translate word for word. Psalm 17:8 pleads for God to "keep me as the apple of your eye." But the actual Hebrew is "keep me as a little man of a daughter of an eye," which would make no sense in English. So no English translations have *ever* rendered this verse literally from the Hebrew. Instead, they understand that the "daughter of an eye" refers to the smaller, delicate part of the eye, the pupil. The Hebrew says nothing about an apple.

Discussions about translation approaches are good to have, since we can never be too careful about reliable translation. Still, most Christians in history knew only one Bible, and if there were problems in the wording of a translation—such as in the Latin Vulgate—the reader was unaware. So we should point out that our concern for translation methods is a blessing. Since we have more than one translation, we have the luxury of debating which method is best. This is a rich legacy. But we should not allow debate over method to cloud the story of the Bible.

The second question Christians today often have is whether the Bible is *trustworthy*. Is the text corrupted, and who determined the books in our Bible? This debate too is a modern one. We will address many of these issues in our first five chapters.

We should start by clarifying the issue. Most questions stem from the fact that certain books were disputed in the early church. Not always and certainly not everywhere, but they were disputed. Eventually someone had to pick the books of the Bible—or so it seems. In popular culture, it has become normal to hear claims that make it sound like the Bible was stitched together by men in a smoky room with the curtains drawn.

These claims have grown in recent years. But it is important to stick to the evidence. In the Old Testament, only a few books were ever disputed—Esther, Ecclesiastes, Song of Songs, and possibly Proverbs. Each of these disputes was related to uncertainty of authorship. The Israelites did not choose random texts for the Old Testament, but instead based each one's inclusion on its authorization by God's chosen prophets or leaders. Because of the uncertain authorship of these few books, the debate was understandable. Only a few books of the New Testament were disputed, such as James, Jude, 2 Peter, and 2 and 3 John.[7] But the vast majority of New Testament books were clearly recognized as inspired Scripture and thus part of the Bible. To put this in perspective, roughly 11 of the 260 chapters of the New Testament were disputed. We will say more about this in chapters 4 and 5.

For now, realize that these questions are focused on the *biblical canon*. In Greek, a canon is a "rule," or "measure," and was a way to determine accuracy. When we use a ruler, for example, there is a standard that keeps the measurements consistent. So any debate about the canon is focused on what *standards* were used when the Bible's books were received as Scripture. The church never canonized books by its own authority; instead, it recognized books' inspiration and canonicity, and it had a functioning canon long before it attempted to define the canon.

Related to canonicity is the issue of the reliability of our copies of the Bible. We've all played the telephone game and know how words can get corrupted. So how can we be confident that the copies of the Old and New Testaments upon which our English Bible translations are based are accurate?

In the Reformation era, European scholars had a smaller number of biblical manuscripts, or copies of the Hebrew Old Testament and Greek New Testament books, than have been found today. Their best copy of the New Testament, for example, dated from the twelfth century. After the rise of archaeology in the nineteenth century, we began to discover *older* copies of the New Testament. From these older copies, we learned that a certain few verses in Bible translations were not likely in the autographs, or original writings of Scripture.

For example, the twelfth-century copy of John 5:4 reads:

> For an angel came down at certain times into the pool and stirred the water: so the first one who entered after the stirring of the water became healed of whatever disease he had. (author transl.)

Older copies of John do *not* have these words, meaning they were not likely in the Gospel as originally written by the apostle John.

Scholars who study biblical manuscripts in order to reconstruct the autographs as closely as possible are known as textual critics. They spend long hours wading through manuscripts to understand how the Bible was copied over the centuries. What is clear from their research is not how corrupt the Bible became over time, but rather how well preserved it is. The text of our Bibles is much more well attested than most ancient books, and we can trust its reliability.

Our Plan

This book will survey thousands of years in only a few pages. For that reason, we hope to be forgiven for not saying everything. Instead, we want to give you the story of the Bible. Indeed, the idea of a *story* is perhaps the best way to approach this book. It is a *biography* of your modern Bible—how it was shaped into the Old and New Testaments, how it was preserved, and the long history of how it was translated into other languages.

However, two things should be said before you begin.

First, this book will not cover every issue in the history of the Bible. And the issues we do raise will be only an introduction. When we discuss the canon of the Bible again, for example, we will not spend an entire chapter arguing over the relevant issues. One of us has already published a book on the canon[8]—and we will recommend further reading on the subject if you want more. Instead, we will stick to the essentials. Our goal is to survey the long history of the Bible with the hope of encouraging you to continue exploring.

Second, this book focuses a great deal on the Bible in the West—especially the story of the English Bible. We do not, however, assume this is the only important story worth exploring. We do this because we are English speakers and so, like many of our readers, we live in a world shaped by the KJV, the NIV, and other translations. But it is impossible for us to cover the explosion of Bible translations in the twentieth century alone. Today, in fact, there are hundreds of translations of the Bible into other languages—and many translation efforts are under way around the globe. All of this should be celebrated and inspire others to tell the story of the Bible in their language.

Study Questions

1. What questions do you have about the Bible before you read this book?
2. How many different translations of the Bible do you own?

Recommended Reading

Arnold, Clinton E. *How We Got the Bible: A Visual Journey.* Grand Rapids: Zondervan, 2008.

Comfort, Philip W., ed. *The Origin of the Bible.* Carol Stream, IL: Tyndale, 2013.

Lightfoot, Neil. *How We Got the Bible.* Grand Rapids: Baker Academic, 2010.

Packer, J. I. *God Has Spoken: Revelation and the Bible.* Grand Rapids: Baker Academic, 1994.

CHAPTER 2

THE OLD TESTAMENT

As the New Testament was being written, the Jews already possessed books written by the inspiration of the Holy Spirit. Christians would eventually call this the *Old Testament*, but nothing in this name should imply these books are worthless or outdated. In fact, the church has always embraced its Jewish foundation. Rather, the Old Testament refers to the *old covenant* God made with Israel. This written covenant, fulfilled by the work of Christ, stretched back centuries to the time of Moses, and even long before that to events recorded in Genesis.

The Old Testament Manuscripts

Any modern discussion of the Old Testament must begin with the copies of the Old Testament we have today. The long history of the preservation, or transmission, of the Bible was important for Christians, especially after the Renaissance (1350–1550) when the study of Hebrew became an essential subject for scholars. Before then, Christians had almost entirely forgotten the language. Jerome was perhaps the last great Hebrew scholar before the Renaissance. A few scholars over the centuries learned the rudiments of Hebrew, often through a rabbi or Jewish community in their region of Europe, but this was exceedingly rare.

The copying of the Old Testament over the centuries, therefore, was done by Jewish scribes. The problem for scholars today, however, is that Jerusalem was destroyed in AD 70. Much was lost in the conflagration, including what must have been a wealth of biblical manuscripts. In fact, the text of our Old Testament is based on copies made in the Middle Ages.

How can we be sure the text of our Old Testament is accurate? The truth is, we do not have a lot of archaeological evidence or manuscripts from the centuries between the destruction of Jerusalem and the Middle Ages. Some manuscripts were lost to the ravages of time, and many of those that remained may have been lost during the Holocaust of World War II.

The best-known period of Hebrew copying was the Masoretic tradition. These were a family of scribes who worked to improve the quality of Bible manuscripts, as well as to ensure consistency for all future copies. The Masoretes flourished from roughly the sixth to the tenth centuries AD, the most famous of whom was the ben Asher family.

Their role in preserving the Bible cannot be overstated, since the Masoretes were the link between earlier versions of the Old Testament, now mostly lost, and the medieval copies of the Hebrew Bible used today when scholars translate the Bible.

The Masoretes were not merely copyists but a community that strove to aid future generations by adding a vowel system to the text, as well as cantillation marks, telling the reader what clauses go together, where to pause, and so forth. In its original form, the Hebrew language was written using only the consonants of each word—a pattern still in practice in modern Israel, where the vowels are not typically written. Those who know Hebrew (and their Bibles) find it natural to read the language this way—just as you know what we mean if we text you that dinner was "rlly gd." The Masoretic texts of the Old Testament, however, included a new vowel system, which was a series of notations above, alongside, and below the consonants that indicate the missing vowels. And for this invention, all new students of Hebrew rise up and call the Masoretes blessed!

Today we have several important copies, the backbone to our Bibles, all made during the Middle Ages. Two of the most important are the Aleppo and Leningrad Codices. Both come from the Masoretic tradition: the Aleppo Codex is older but incomplete since it was damaged in a fire in 1947 and lacks portions of the Torah. Both are written in book form (*codex*) and not on scrolls. By far, the most important manuscript is the Leningrad Codex—named for the fact that it is housed at the Russian National Library. All significant editions of the Hebrew Bible today are based primarily on the Leningrad Codex, since it is the oldest complete manuscript of the Old Testament.

But perhaps the most important archaeological discovery ever gave us new insights into the Old Testament. In 1946, a Bedouin shepherd was tending his flocks near the city of Qumran—an arid region in the West Bank, remembered by Bible students as the location where David fled from Saul. Breaking open several jars, the shepherd found scrolls that appeared to be copies of the Bible (although the shepherd did not know this at the time). Several years later—after dealer reaction was lukewarm—archaeologists at the Hebrew University of Jerusalem became aware of these scrolls and launched a search for the caves. On January 28, 1949, the first cave of the Qumran community was opened, and as of 2017 a total of twelve caves have been discovered.

The discovery is known today as the *Dead Sea Scrolls*—though it may be fitting to describe it as the Dead Sea Caves since the excavation focused on opening and exploring at least a dozen locations, hidden for centuries after the fall of Jerusalem. The caves were filled with jars containing scrolls with a wide variety of biblical and extrabiblical texts. Suddenly, scholars had Hebrew fragments (or even large samples, and a complete copy of Isaiah) of books of the Old Testament that dated from 250 to 65 BC. Now it was possible to compare these older versions to the scribal tradition of the Leningrad Codex—an improvement of almost a thousand years.

This discovery not only validated the painstaking work of the Masoretic scribes but also showed that their predecessors, the scribes who over the centuries had copied the Old Testament, had preserved the text accurately. All the texts of our Old Testament were at Qumran except Esther. There are slight differences in the texts of Qumran—not unlike when scholars find slight differences between copies of the New Testament—but those differences amount to roughly a 1 percent discrepancy between the Masoretic text and these ancient texts. In a few cases, the scrolls even *restored* verses that had been lost—such as Psalm 145:13 ("The LORD is trustworthy in all he promises / and faithful in all he does"). These last two lines had only one Masoretic witness, and so were often left out of earlier translations, but the scrolls of Qumran showed they were original.[1]

In the end, the best way to understand the Qumran texts is to realize how remarkably well the Old Testament has been preserved over the centuries—a fact that speaks to God's preservation of his Word but also to the faithfulness of those who copied it. The Hebrew texts used to translate our modern Old Testament, therefore, are trustworthy.

The Torah

Despite the discoveries at Qumran, the fact that our Old Testament manuscripts are based on medieval copies can provoke questions. Is the Jewish Bible the same as our Christian Old Testament? The answer is yes and no—yes regarding *content*, but no regarding *form*. All of the books of the Jewish Bible are published in modern Protestant Bibles; their content is the same.

If we were to travel back to the time of the Old Testament, we would find that the most significant difference between the Jewish Bible and the modern Old Testament is actually their *arrangement*.

The formation of the Old Testament begins with leaders sent by God to proclaim his Word. These were leaders of Israel, especially prophets, who were called and appointed directly by God. The first evidence we have of the writing of the Old Testament is Moses. Though Genesis is set before the calling of Moses—with the narrative of creation and the fall, Noah, and Abraham's lineage— these stories probably were written or remembered through oral tradition. But with the calling of Moses, God entered into a new relationship with Israel, instructing Moses to write down everything God commanded. The account in Exodus, therefore, forms the crucial moment in the formation of these five books—also known as the Pentateuch (*Five Books*).[2]

These five books were always arranged in the same order: Genesis, Exodus, Leviticus, Numbers, Deuteronomy. For the Jews, the collection was known as the *Torah*, or the *Teaching*—an inclusive word that means the entirety of these books, not simply the Ten Commandments or other laws. Moses was the principal author of the Torah, save a few passages, such as the recording of his death in Deuteronomy 34.[3]

The heart of the Torah is in the story of Exodus and God's covenant at Sinai. In some respects, the Torah was considered the basis for the rest of the Old Testament, though the Jews did not consider the latter books to have less authority or inspiration. Rather, the Torah was the *foundation of the covenant* God made with Israel. Jewish study of the Scriptures always began with the Torah.

By the time of the New Testament, the pharisaical tradition went beyond the text itself and added oral law—a series of 613 rules or applications based on the Torah, some of which we see mentioned in the New Testament, since they form the basis of disputes between Christ and the Pharisees (cf. Matthew 9:14). The Sadducees, by contrast, followed only the Torah, although this does not mean they rejected the rest of the Old Testament, but that they rejected the accompanying oral traditions. All Jews looked to the Torah as the first step in their long history as God's people. Therefore, the Pentateuch has always been the first five books of every Bible.

The Prophets

After the Torah, the Jewish arrangement of the Old Testament differs from our Christian Bibles. In the Jewish canon, the books that came after the Torah were known as the Prophets (*Nevi'im*).[4] Many of these books are not *prophetic* as we use the word in English, but they are the major books that tell of the transition from Moses to the foundation of the kingdom of Israel. This period saw the building of the first temple in Jerusalem.

In the Jewish reckoning, the Nevi'im divides into two sections: the Former Prophets (Joshua, Judges, Samuel, Kings) and the Latter

Prophets (Isaiah, Jeremiah, Ezekiel, and the Minor Prophets). The twenty-one books in our Old Testament are combined into just eight in the Jewish canon, with Samuel and Kings understood as one book each, and the twelve shorter books of prophets combined into a single book. Most of the prophetical books were written before the Babylonian captivity in the 500s BC.

The Writings

The last collection of books in the Jewish canon are known as the Writings (*Ketuvim*)—or sometimes the Holy Writings (*Hagiographa*[5]). These books were not seen as a lesser authority, as if they were simply tacked on later to the Jewish canon. Instead, the subjects they deal with are different, since books like Daniel, Ezra, and Esther focus on the time in Babylon (or shortly after Israel returned), though they give no exact date. But since books like Daniel are not in the earlier prophetic section, does this mean Daniel is not prophecy? No, only that Daniel was written during Israel's time in Babylon. Jesus himself referred to Daniel as a prophet in Matthew 24:15.

Like the Prophets, the books in the Writings were divided into subcategories, three in this case. The first division combines what scholars today call wisdom literature: Job, Psalms, and Proverbs.[6] These books are well known to all Bible students, but none so much as the Psalms, perhaps, which were the lyrical heart of Israelite worship. The next section is called the Five Scrolls (*Hamesh Megillot*), joining the Song of Songs, Ruth, Lamentations, Ecclesiastes, and Esther. The remaining books in the Writings, then, are Daniel, Ezra-Nehemiah, and Chronicles added at the end.

The Tanakh

When we combine each of these parts of the Jewish canon, we get the Tanakh, or the TaNaK—a word formed from the first letter of each section (Torah-Nevi'im-Ketuvim). In other words, the Tanakh is the Jewish canon in its entirety, the same as our Old Testament.

Because the Jewish canon was arranged in this manner, it gave rise to a Jewish shorthand description—namely, "the Law and the Prophets" or "the Law, the Prophets, and the Psalms." A modern reader of the New Testament might be confused by such terminology. The Prophets here refers to the Nevi'im as a whole, and the mention of the Psalms indicates the Ketuvim. These expressions were common Jewish ways, used by Jesus and his disciples, to refer to the full Old Testament.[7]

All of this may seem interesting, but is there a benefit to understanding the Jewish ordering of the Old Testament? We think so. Students of the Bible often find it confusing that the Old Testament is not arranged chronologically—after all, Ezra-Nehemiah, written *after* the return from exile, is placed *before* the prophets who warn Israel that God will send them into exile if they refuse to repent. Imagine trying to understand a book if the final chapter is in the middle! But if we understand the Jewish ordering, it can be a helpful way to remember the history of Israel. Daniel falls in the later Writings, so we remember he served *during* Israel's time in Babylon. Isaiah falls in the Prophets, so we remember he served Israel *before* the exile.

In the end, we have the same Old Testament as the Jews, so we should not be troubled by the different ordering. The Old Testament is a complex and beautiful story, and it can be intimidating to new Christians. There is no silver bullet for easily learning the story of God's dealings with Israel, but it helps to know the original structure of the Hebrew Bible.

The Jewish Canon

How did the Jews recognize that the books of the Old Testament were inspired Scripture? How did they receive these books into their canon?

The first question was whether the author was called directly by God. The books of Moses and the larger and shorter prophetic books clearly fit into this category. They were written or recorded based on the teachings of these Israelite leaders. Other books emerged during the life of Israel—books such as the Psalms, which were developed over time and not written by any one author. But in the Psalms we see evidence of David and others who are credited with having written the bulk of the 150 psalms. Finally, other books record the history of Israel, though we do not have an author's name associated with them. Chronicles and Kings do not provide an author, but they were received as official records of Israel's development after settling in Canaan. So the calling of the author or authors of each book was perhaps the most crucial factor in their reception into the Old Testament, but other factors contributed to recognition of a book's inspiration and canonicity.

It is often said that the Jewish canon was not finalized until the Council of Jamnia in the first century. In fact, this was not a *council* that decided anything, at least not like the Council of Nicaea. Rather, it was a rabbinic center that rose to prominence in the city of Jamnia (or Yavneh) after Jerusalem was destroyed in AD 70. The Jews had long known the canon of the Old Testament, and there were no serious or lasting controversies over any Old Testament books. After Jerusalem was destroyed—and with it copies of the Old Testament and other precious items of history—the group at Jamnia worked to preserve their Jewish heritage. Part of that heritage was ensuring that the canon of the Old Testament was not forgotten. The point of any discussions was not to *determine* the canon but to *affirm* what was already authoritative for the community.

The only debate among the rabbis at Jamnia was over a few disputed books. Why the debate? The answer is that, while the Jews had a collection of inspired books, they also treasured other books that told the stories of the wider Jewish heritage. The books of I and II Maccabees, for example, told the story of Judah Maccabee and the resistance to the legislation in favor of Greek paganism by Antiochus IV. This story formed the background to the celebration of Hanukkah, when the Jews retook the temple. These books were vital to the Jews, but they had never been part of the Old Testament. Several of these books were included, therefore, in the Septuagint translation of the Old Testament—which we will look at in our next chapter. They were important books, but not part of the Bible.

Conclusion

As we mentioned earlier in this chapter, the content of the Old Testament has remained the same, though the arrangement of the books is different in the Jewish Bible. The authority of the Old Testament was doubted neither by Christians nor by Jews at the time of Christ's birth. The historian Josephus, for example, wrote of the Old Testament that "although such long ages have gone by, no one has dared to add anything to them, to take away anything in them, or to change anything in them."[8]

The New Testament authors echoed this commitment to the authority of the Old Testament, affirming that the Israelites were given God's Word and thus Christians too must receive the Old Testament books as Scripture (cf. 2 Timothy 3:16; Hebrews 1:1; 2 Peter 1:20–21).

Study Questions

1. Write down the division of Torah, Prophets, and Writings, and which books the Jews included in each group.
2. Why was the Qumran discovery significant?
3. What contributions did the Masoretes bring to the Hebrew Bible? What were their motivations?
4. Describe how the canon of the Old Testament was established. How did Israel determine if someone had the right to speak for God?
5. In what ways did this study strengthen your trust in the reliability of the transmitted text?

Recommended Reading

Alexander, T. Desmond. *From Paradise to the Promised Land: An Introduction to the Pentateuch*. Grand Rapids: Baker Academic, 2012.

DeRouchie, Jason S. *What the Old Testament Authors Really Cared About: A Survey of Jesus' Bible*. Grand Rapids: Kregel, 2013.

Van Pelt, Miles, ed. *A Biblical-Theological Introduction to the Old Testament*. Wheaton, IL: Crossway, 2016.

CHAPTER 3

THE SEPTUAGINT AND THE APOCRYPHA

The Jewish people suffered the destruction of Jerusalem in the year AD 70. Angered over centuries of foreign oppression, and seeking to cast off the Romans, many Jews rose in a rebellion around the year 66. With the Romans, few things raised their bloodlust more than rebellion. The empire believed it had been charitable toward Israel; they expected the Jews to be grateful. To now see the haughty eyes of their subjects as they rose in revolt—this was the last straw.

Roman legions marched into Jerusalem and destroyed it, removing every stone from the temple. The Wailing Wall that still stands today, in fact, is not part of the original structure but a retaining wall located near the Temple Mount. The Romans also ordered the Jews never to return to Jerusalem and gave the city a pagan name. Those who visit Rome today can see the Arch of Titus, commissioned in honor of the Roman destruction of Jerusalem. Carved into its stone are soldiers carrying a menorah, silver trumpets, and other spoils taken from the temple.

Shattered and exiled, many Jews were forced out of their

homeland, capping off centuries of migration known as the *Jewish Diaspora*. The Jews who settled elsewhere eventually spoke new languages, and so they needed a new translation of the Bible. This spread of Jewish culture led to the first translation of the Old Testament.

The Greek World

Centuries before the birth of Christ, the Jews living outside of Jerusalem became increasingly dependent on the Greek language for everyday life.[1] Though the Hebrew language was their heritage, and though the Hebrew text was read in the synagogues, everyday life was being overtaken by Greek.

Why? The single most influential factor was the conquests of Alexander the Great in the fourth century BC. A Macedonian by birth, Alexander launched an eastward campaign to conquer most of the lands between Greece and India. He died in 323 BC, but Alexander left a kingdom that reached from Greece, down into the Palestinian and Egyptian regions, and over to the Himalaya mountains. Those who served with Alexander, however, were unprepared for his sudden death, and their struggle to claim these lands resulted in the breakup of Alexander's lands into four territories: the kingdoms of Ptolemy, Seleucus, Pergamum, and Macedon. Each was run by men who were Greek in culture and language, forcing local communities to adapt to their new Greek masters.

Greek influence was not a small factor in the ancient world. Lands had their own native language, culture, and religion, but they were now ruled by the Greeks. Locals who wanted to advance in status under the Greeks had to adapt to the new language and customs. Within several generations, Greek culture was displacing native languages as texts, inscriptions, and other features of the Near East began increasingly to use Greek.[2]

Perhaps the most influential city that embodied the spread of Greek culture took its name from the conquering Alexander: the Egyptian city of Alexandria. Legends tempt scholars and historians with stories of the Library of Alexandria, now lost, once brimming with scrolls and codices of ancient texts. Many of the world's greatest philosophers—including those from Judaism and Christianity—found their way to the city. For centuries, the cultural power of Alexandria was a symbol of the influence of the Greeks.

These Greek influences, as well as later Roman influence, created what we call the *Greco-Roman world*. The most enduring legacy was the Greek language, which even the Roman Empire continued to use as a language of trade and culture. Much like French in the nineteenth century or English in the twentieth century, Greek became a prestige language. Indeed, so pervasive was the cultural influence of the Greeks that knowledge of Greek spilled down onto the streets, creating a "common" (*koine*) or simplified form of Greek used in the marketplace. Most of the New Testament books were written in this Koine Greek, and the choice to write in Greek was no accident. Centuries of development and expansion of Greek culture and values contributed to the need to communicate in a language understood by people throughout the Mediterranean.

The New Testament was not the first example of God's Word being communicated through Greek. The same impact of Greek had been felt for centuries by the Jews, especially in those regions beyond the heartland of Jerusalem. Within a century of the Alexandrian conquests, the Jews thought it necessary to translate their Scriptures into Greek.

Legends of the Seventy

How did the Greek translation of the Old Testament come about? One of the enduring stories of the Septuagint is the legend of its creation.[3] In the Letter of Aristeas, a story is told of the king of Egypt, Ptolemy II Philadelphus (285–246 BC). The collections in his library were splendid, though his librarian, Demetrius, lobbied to have included the essential Scriptures of the Jews. Ptolemy was pleased by this idea, and he sent a delegation (including Aristeas) to ask the high priest in Jerusalem for a translation of the Torah. The Jews agreed and selected seventy-two scribes, placing them in separate chambers and asking them to translate the Torah. Miraculously, the translations came out identical—an indication of the scribes' knowledge of the Hebrew and God's providence over the creation of the Septuagint.

The Letter of Aristeas was forged by someone other than the real Aristeas. But the story was picked up by several influential writers—Philo of Alexandria for the Jews and Augustine for later Christians—and became a simplified explanation for the Septuagint. The fable also gave us the name of the translation, since *septuaginta* was Greek for "seventy"—thus the work of the seventy scribal translators. For this reason, books will often use the shorthand Roman numeral LXX to refer to the Septuagint. But these miracles and legends were later inventions to bolster the Septuagint translation—something that sometimes occurs when a version of the Bible is cherished for centuries.[4] These myths may seem silly today—and they are easily refuted—but the translations themselves are sound, and they give us vital links to the days between the Old and New Testaments.

The Septuagint, however, even without these stories, was still significant. The city of Alexandria was the center of the Jewish scholars, since the city was densely populated by Jewish emigrants—making up as much as a third of the city. There was pressure to accomodate Hebrew culture to the Greek culture of the city, especially for younger generations. Since the Jews needed God's Word, the inability of some to understand the Bible was too high a risk. The first portion translated was the Torah, and though we are uncertain of the date it was translated, we begin to see citations of these passages in Greek by the middle of the second century BC. The translation work continued, and thus, by the birth of Christ, we can be confident of the presence of at least some version of a complete Septuagint. The authors of the New Testament likely knew the Septuagint well.

It is essential to understand that the Septuagint was translated over centuries, by a variety of translators. The Septuagint was not a single translation—as we may think of the modern New International Version (NIV) or the Revised Standard Version (RSV). We have around two thousand manuscripts or fragments that are classified as the Septuagint, though most of the ancient copies have been lost. So when we describe the role of the Septuagint, we mean the influence of the Greek Old Testament *in general*.[5]

Since it was the oldest translation of the Hebrew text, the Septuagint provides us an opportunity to explore interpretation of the Old Testament in the centuries before the New Testament. When this is combined with the study of other ancient translations into Syriac, Coptic, Ethiopian, Old Latin, and other languages, our understanding of the shades of meaning in the Old Testament increases in complexity and richness. We can explore the history of the Bible through multiple languages, all written centuries ago.

Today scholars work with these remaining manuscripts to see if they can fathom the different instincts of the translators. Why were certain word choices preferred over others, for example? There are also some passages that are abbreviated from the original Hebrew. As we noted in chapter 1, all translations of the Bible use one of two methods in bringing the text into a new langauge. With the Septuagint texts, it is best to see that there are different methodologies at work. Some of the translations are debated today—such as the wording of Isaiah 7:14 that "the virgin will conceive," since the Hebrew can also be translated "the young girl will conceive." The Septuagint chose "virgin." The difference is somewhat inconsequential: a young girl would also be a virgin. But centuries after it was translated, the Septuagint continues to influence how we study the Bible.

There are other influences of the Septuagint on our Bibles. Perhaps the most important is the arrangement of its books. At some point, those who copied the Septuagint rearranged the books, moving books from the Writings (Ketuvim) to the Prophets (Nevi'im). For example, Ruth was placed after Judges to make the relationship between these books clear, since the timeline of the two coincided. All the historical books, including Chronicles, were grouped. Also grouped were all the books of wisdom literature, rather than being arranged separately, some in the Prophets and some in the Writings. The books that remain are the prophets (as we use the term today), though their arrangement was different: the Septuagint grouped the twelve minor prophets first, followed by the major prophets. The book of Daniel was then placed at the end.

Our Old Testament eventually came to follow this same pattern, though not to the letter. Like the Septuagint, our Bibles have the historical books and wisdom literature together. Ezra and Nehemiah were written toward the end of the Israelite period, after the Babylonian exile, but are placed in the middle of our Old Testament to complete the historical books. Not surprisingly, new students of the Bible often say that the arrangement of our Old Testament *appears* to be out of order, when actually the books are arranged by genre—just as they were in the Septuagint. The prophetic books of the Old Testament are arranged in the order of the Septuagint, but in reverse; the longer prophets like Isaiah come first, followed by the minor prophets.

Some Jewish texts outside the canon were included in copies of the Septuagint. We are unsure if these texts were simply kept together with the Bible or if some had erroneously come to view these books as part of the Old Testament. These books, such as I and II Maccabees, were culturally significant. Other works were supplements to books of the Old Testament—with two additions to Daniel and one to Esther, as well as the *Epistle of Jeremiah*. A Psalm 151 was also added to the Septuagint. All these texts and a few more would later be dubbed *deuterocanonical*, meaning they were never part of the original Scripture, thus making them a *secondary*, or lesser, *canon*. We will look at this in more detail in chapter 5.

In Christian history, some of these books would become known as the Apocrypha—included in Catholic and Orthodox Scriptures but not in Protestant versions. The reason they became associated with the Old Testament was mainly due to the influence of the Septuagint.

The Influence of the Septuagint

The Septuagint played a decisive role in the early church. The need for a Greek translation was felt in several communities of early Christians—especially those with no Jewish converts who retained the knowledge of Hebrew. As time wore on, the use of the Septuagint spread. Still, the influence of the Septuagint was felt especially in the Eastern church, later known as the Orthodox Church, which to this day maintains the Septuagint as its Scriptures.

However, some rejected the Septuagint. New translations are often a nuisance: one translation is read for centuries, but when flaws are noticed in the translation, a battle erupts over the translation's quality. So it was with the Septuagint. Not a few Jews resisted the popularity of the Septuagint. The primary reason for this was the loss of Hebraic culture—not least because Greek was a language spread to the Jews by their oppressors.

We see this tension in the New Testament, with the calling of the first deacons in Acts 6. The first verse says that the "Hellenistic Jews . . . complained against the Hebraic Jews because their widows were being overlooked in the daily distribution of food." The Hellenists were, in fact, those Jews who were Greek-speaking; they would have been people who used the Septuagint. Paul's language in Philippians 3:5—recounting his former life as a "Hebrew of Hebrews"—perhaps echoes the same idea that Paul believed he was undefiled by any adoption of Greek culture.

After the destruction of Jerusalem, however, there seems to have been a sudden tilt back in favor of the Hebrew version for Jews. This led to at least a few embarrassing debates between early Christians and Jews. For example, early Christians at times cited books from the Apocrypha, which the Jews did not consider part of the Bible. The early theologian Origen unearthed this problem when he moved to Caesarea, where he found a thriving community of Hebrew-speaking Jews. He was left with a conundrum:

Should people go back to the Jewish canon or continue to use the Septuagint, with its additional texts? Origen argued in favor of the Septuagint. There was no urgency, he felt, in changing the Bible used by most churches. Why stress the problem to such an extent that it caused division?

But it was still embarrassing to cite books the Jews did not recognize. In the end, Origen sought for a harmony between the Septuagint and the original Hebrew canon. The Septuagint was a translation, but it was not a bad one:

> I have tried to repair the disagreements in the copies of the Old Testament on the basis of the other versions. When I was uncertain of the Septuagint reading, . . . I settled the issue by consulting the other versions and retaining what was in agreement with them. . . . Those who wish to, may accept them; anyone who is offended by this procedure may accept or reject them as he chooses.[6]

The only problem here is that Origen essentially admits the Septuagint is *inferior* to the original Hebrew text—or at least not word for word in step with the Hebrew Old Testament. Yet he also claimed the Septuagint was given to the church *by God's providence*. Origen was hoping for a way to maintain the *authority* of the Septuagint while also working to correct issues in the text according to the original Hebrew.

Conclusion

As we have seen so far in our story, widely used translations have power. When a single translation is used over decades (or centuries), its influence is magnified. But the influence of popular translations tends to create problems for later scholars who find improvements that need to be made to the translation. This is not a modern problem. This pattern was already at work in the increased popularity of the Septuagint in the life of the church, and by the time of Jerome in the fourth century, the use of the Septuagint was widespread enough that his return to the original Hebrew as the basis of the Vulgate was considered shameful by some.

Study Questions

1. Why did the Jews translate the Old Testament from Hebrew to Greek?
2. What is the Old Testament Apocrypha, and where did it come from?
3. In what ways did the Septuagint influence the early church?
4. What problems were there in the use of the Septuagint by early Christians?

Recommended Reading

Jobes, Karen, and Moisés Silva. *Invitation to the Septuagint*. 2nd ed. Grand Rapids: Baker Academic, 2015.

CHAPTER 4

THE NEW TESTAMENT

Each of Jesus's disciples was raised to confess the one true God of Israel. In particular, a single Old Testament verse came to be the heart of this confession, Deuteronomy 6:4: "Hear, O Israel: The LORD our God, the LORD is one." For Israel, these words lie at the heart of their understanding of God.

Why is this? Part of the answer is the world of Israel, since they lived so near pagan nations with their own religions. Of all the things that separated Israel from other nations, few were more important than their confession that God alone is the Creator. In the ancient world, most religions believed in multiple deities. Each of these gods had a role—giving blessings or curses—and they often required certain sacrifices before responding to humans.

By contrast, the biblical faith was not based on sacrifices to *earn* the favors of the gods. Instead, the Jews worshiped the God of heaven and earth—the same God who had *rescued them* from Egypt, *carried them* to Sinai, and *blessed them* long before any covenant had been ratified. In the ancient world, the Jewish faith was set apart, never to accept foreign gods. They did not always obey, but God always called on them to give up these false gods and return to faith in the true God.

In the New Testament, God himself came in the person of Jesus Christ. The divine identity of Christ—that he was with God and was God—is affirmed in the Gospels (e.g., John 1). The fact that Christ is Lord is declared in every New Testament book. Even more startling, Jesus *accepted* the worship and obedience of his followers, a scandalous act for many Jews, who saw Jesus as a blasphemer. Jesus also spoke *of the Father* and *of the Holy Spirit* in a way that distinguished them—saying he would go to his Father and that he would send the Spirit. Likewise, the Father spoke *of the Son* during the baptism of Jesus, telling the Jews to listen to him, as the Holy Spirit descended like a dove.[1]

The disciples still worshiped one God—only God was speaking of himself using three separate *pronouns*, or what the church later would define as three *persons*.[2] One God, three voices, three persons.

This unique moment in the life of God's people—Jesus's incarnation, the sending of the Holy Spirit, and all the implications of both for the church—is at the heart of the New Testament. In this chapter, we will explore how the New Testament was formed (looking especially at the sending of the apostles) and what factors led the church to receive it as God's Word. How did the early church know which books were truly from God? As with the Old Testament, we will also say a few things about how the New Testament is arranged in our Bible.

The Holy Spirit Restored

One of the features of the New Testament that is often overlooked is the restoration of the Holy Spirit after the close of the Old Testament canon. As we saw in our previous chapters, the disobedience of Israel eventually led to the Babylonian exile. In a dramatic moment for Israel, Ezekiel 8–11 shows the glory of the Lord departing from the temple. This was a sign not only of God's withdrawing his presence from Israel but also of the coming judgment in exile. After suffering in slavery, the Israelites returned home, and God again sent leaders and prophets—specifically Malachi, Ezra, and Nehemiah—who called on Israel to repent and return to the covenant. For a season, the stubborn defiance against God receded. The zeal to obey God returned, especially when the Law was recovered and read to the nation (Nehemiah 8). But after this season, with Israel still only lukewarm, God no longer sent prophets to Israel.

We do not want to overstate the case. It would be wrong to say that God was utterly *silent* after Israel returned from exile—as if his commands were not already set down in the Old Testament or as if he ceased to care for Israel. But even in Jewish traditions, there arose the belief that God had stopped calling prophets and spiritual leaders as he had in the Old Testament period. This was a spiritual famine, they argued, for their wickedness. In a later Jewish tradition called the Talmud, the rabbis offered a sobering comment:

> Just as little remains from a cedar tree infested with this worm, so too all that remained of the Divine Presence during the Second Temple period was a Divine Voice, as it was taught in the *baraita* . . . which they heard as an echo of prophecy.[3]

The "Second Temple period" here means the time between the Old and New Testaments. Also, the *"echo of prophecy"* here means the oral law—the *baraita*—that began to develop prior to the birth of Christ. We see some of this tradition in the practices of the Sadducees and Pharisees in the Gospels. But this statement is somber—almost grievous. Because of their sins, God ceased to speak directly to his people. All that remained, between Malachi and the New Testament, was an echo.

An important aspect of this problem for Israel is it explains what Jesus was doing by sending his apostles.[4] For example, Luke 24:47 tells how Jesus embraced an important message for his earthly ministry—that "repentance for the forgiveness of sins will be preached in his name to all nations, beginning at Jerusalem." These words refer to Isaiah 2, where God told Israel prior to the exile that "the word of the LORD [will go out] from Jerusalem" (v. 3). During the exile and judgment on Israel, however, it seemed that God's Word would never return to Jerusalem, much less spread from there to the ends of the earth.

So by the time of the New Testament, the Jews had a clear understanding that the coming Messiah would *restore* the Word of God to Israel, first in Jerusalem and then flowing out to the world. Jesus regularly proclaimed to his disciples and the wider public that the hope of Israel was fulfilled in his coming. *Now* the Word was back, *now* God spoke to his people—only not through a prophet but directly, in the person of Christ. Israel was to rejoice. Also important, however, was the sending of the apostles to God's people—which was the sending of authorized witnesses to proclaim the good news.

The coming of Christ, therefore, was not just the manifestation of God's kingdom. Nor was it simply about bringing personal salvation. It was also the *restoration* of the Holy Spirit to God's people. This fulfillment of the Old Testament is, in part, why the rejection of Jesus by many in Israel is described as their willful ignorance of the Old Testament. They refused to see that salvation was to begin with Israel, but God wanted his Word throughout the earth.

Christ tells them of their insensitivity to the work of the Spirit. Their *eyes and ears were closed*, and Israel was called *stiff-necked*, a people whose hearts were uncircumcised. All of this language speaks to their hard-heartedness toward the return of the Spirit.[5] Those who placed their faith in Jesus, however, experienced overwhelming joy in Acts 2—the prophecy of Joel was fulfilled, and God poured out his Spirit on all flesh. God had not only restored his people but also given them an abundance of his presence in the Holy Spirit.

The New Testament period began, therefore, with a dramatic awareness among the Jews that Israel needed this restoration if they were to reach the nations.

For now, all we need to know is that there is a connection between (1) God restoring the Holy Spirit to his people and (2) the coming of another time of God's revelation. In other words, the assumption was that, if God restored the Holy Spirit, then it was only natural to conclude this would include other writings for the Bible canon—just as the writings of Old Testament prophets and leaders were collected in the Old Testament. There were no assumptions as to how this would look, but it was believed that God had restored Israel. And that restoration meant the return of God's revelation.

The Arrangement of the New Testament

It is impossible to determine with absolute precision the date or location of the writing of every book in the New Testament. There are numerous suggestions for the dating of each book, though they are often given a range of possible dates. With Paul's letters, compared with the stories in Acts, we have reasonable evidence as to when they were written. But other books, like Hebrews or James, give us no clues about date or location. Instead, what we have are traditions recounted in the early church about most of the New Testament books.

The formation of the New Testament is important. We can begin with how the books of the New Testament were arranged. As with the Old Testament canon, the arrangement of the New Testament books is not necessarily based on the general date of their writing. Instead, the twenty-seven books are arranged according to *genre*, and then often according to *size*. In every Bible we know of, the Gospels come first—based on the fact that Christ's ministry is the foundation of the new covenant. In modern Bibles, the Gospels are then followed by Acts, the epistles of Paul, the remaining epistles of Hebrews, James, Peter, John, and Jude, and finally Revelation.

The New Testament begins, then, with the four canonical Gospels. Each tells the story of the life, death, and resurrection of Christ—although each has different focal points or emphases in the story. We are not sure which of the Gospels was written first, and even though many scholars believe Mark was the earliest, there are possible reasons to believe Matthew or Luke may have been first. Whatever the case, the three first Gospels—Matthew, Mark, and Luke—form a unit that scholars call the *Synoptic Gospels*. The word *synoptic* is borrowed from the Greek and refers to things *seen or viewed together*[6]—so in this case, the word refers to the fact that students of the Gospels often see these three books as working together, probably even using one another in their composition.

The surest conclusion—based largely on the witness of the early church—is that John was the last Gospel. Of the four Gospels, John is exceptional in style and focus. The writing is profound yet straightforward—with short sentences and basic syntax. However, *simple* does not mean that John is *simplistic*. For example, the opening verses state some of the most profound concepts about the Word who "was God" and "was with God," who came and took on human flesh (John 1:1–2, 14). The Gospel of John also focuses on some of the most intimate moments in Jesus's life, such as his prayer the night before the crucifixion (John 17).

After the Gospels is the book of Acts, written by Luke. For this reason, many often describe *Luke-Acts* as one unit, with Acts picking up after Jesus's resurrection, carrying the story into the early life of the church. Some of the features of Acts tell us about the changes made in the ancient church—such as the calling of the first deacons—though most of the book focuses on the ministry of Paul and the spread of the gospel to the gentiles.

Paul's letters form the majority of the New Testament. But like the prophetic books of the Old Testament, they are arranged according to their *size* (the only exception being that 2 Corinthians is placed after 1 Corinthians). Each of these books is a letter from Paul, written to churches or individuals, usually to address issues in the local church. For example, the division in Corinth provoked the writing of 1 Corinthians, while confusion over adherence to Jewish custom—which some believed was mandatory—inspired Galatians.

The final letters of Paul cover a variety of topics, among the most important being Paul's instructions for the selection of elders to govern local churches. These letters were written at the end of Paul's ministry and bear witness to the ordering of the church as the apostles were approaching the end of their lives.

Hebrews is the longest of the latter letters. In the early church—and through much of the Middle Ages—Hebrews was assumed to be a work of Paul (why some accounts say that Paul had fourteen letters). No author is mentioned in the book, so the suggestion that Paul wrote it was only guesswork, though once it was assumed, this view became widespread. By the Renaissance, however, and certainly by the Reformation, it was clear the writer could not conclusively be identified as Paul. Many scholars today believe that Hebrews, due to its style of writing, was based on a spoken exhortation to a Christian community—perhaps a community undergoing suffering (Hebrews 12).

The final letters of the New Testament are James, two epistles from Peter, three epistles from John, and Jude. These letters are often referred to as the Catholic Epistles—not because they are used only by Roman Catholics but because their intended audience seems to be the *universal* (viz. *catholic*) church. The New Testament concludes with the vision of John in the book of Revelation, with its soaring conclusion in chapters 21 and 22 of the new heaven and new earth—the final act of redemption when Christ returns.

The Authority of the New Testament

A final word can be said about the apostolic authority of the books in the New Testament. Given that many of the books of the New Testament are letters—written to specific churches—it may seem natural to conclude that the apostles did not realize these texts would be scriptural. Did they know these works were going to be collected and included in the Bible? Maybe they just wrote letters, and the early church created a Bible out of them.

To answer this question, we must understand the apostolic sense of calling that is found throughout the New Testament.

Christ had called and sent his apostles to bear witness to his kingdom. Naturally, the apostles had a profound understanding of this authority. We can take Paul as an example. In 2 Corinthians 3:6, Paul refers to himself and, by extension, the other apostles as "ministers of a new covenant." He writes that his ministry is inspired directly by the Spirit (vv. 6, 8) and that his calling is a "ministry of reconciliation" (2 Corinthians 5:18). This is important, because later in chapter 5 he refers to the "message of reconciliation" (v. 19) he and the other apostles have been entrusted with. He even declares that "Christ is speaking through me" (13:3) as he writes the letter. In other words, Paul does not consider his words to be merely a casual letter—or even just an important pastoral letter. The message he delivers, both in his preaching and in his writing, is *authoritative* in a way that is unique to those who are apostles.

The point to be grasped here is that the church has always understood that God's speech to his people—his Word—is embodied in what may seem humdrum and ordinary, such as a letter from an apostle. The Bible is inspired, yet still reflects the uniqueness of the writers who were sent to proclaim the message. There is no sense that Paul or the other New Testament writers slip in and out of divine proclamation simply because the letters are the works of their own hand—even if their personality is displayed in their writings. God called *people* to deliver his Word, and those people have distinctive personalities, but their words carry a unique authority.

As we saw earlier in this chapter, the return of God's Word was connected to the moment of redemption in Christ. It was assumed that once the Messiah came, God would again send divinely inspired leaders, just as he had in the Old Testament. The apostolic time, in other words, was expected to be only a small window, after which it would close. That window in time was when the apostles were living, when they were still on the initial mission of the church, and before their own disciples began to lead the church.

As long as there were *living apostles,* there was the official proclamation of God's message to his people. No one else was empowered with this calling. This is why Paul tells Galatia that he was an apostle called directly by Christ (Galatians 1:11–12). He makes it clear that he did not need human validation, since his authority as an apostle rested on Christ's calling to be a voice for the gospel. Though some authors of New Testaement books were not themselves apostles, their message was based on their relationship to the apostles, not their own authority.

Apostolic authority was therefore one of the most important issues for the early church. The reception of a book was always based largely on direct apostolic authority—or else the church affirmed the books were written by *apostolic coworkers* like Mark and Luke. This authority was something the church recognized as an internal witness in each New Testament book. The apostles made it clear their words were to be maintained by those who came after, since their words alone carried the authority of the Messiah.

For example, take the book of Hebrews—a book that some allege was received only because it was thought to be the work of Paul. But now that this authorship is rejected, should we reject Hebrews?

No. The church received Hebrews in the canon for the same reason it accepted Mark and Luke. Hebrews was written in the earliest years of the apostolic ministry—indeed, it was already being cited by 1 Clement in the first century. The author describes himself as a companion with Timothy on apostolic journeys (13:23), making him a co-laborer with the apostles, just as Mark and Luke

THE NEW TESTAMENT | 61

were. It is true that the author of Hebrews is unknown, but the candidates for its authorship could only have been from the small number of those who served with the apostles. Its message is clearly based on the *witness* of the apostles, and so, like the rest of the New Testament books, it was received as apostolic.

Conclusion

The New Testament was an outburst of proclamation of God's Word after the coming of Jesus. The apostles (or their companions) who wrote each book did not assume their writings were simply one of a dozen other alternative accounts of the message of God's redemption. The apostles were sent directly by Christ and inspired by the Holy Spirit, and their message held a unique authority over the church—in the same way the prophets and other Old Testament writers wrote God's word for Israel.

Study Questions

1. Roughly at what time did prophets cease to be sent to Israel?
2. Did the apostles see themselves as unique leaders in God's plan? Explain.
3. Must every book of the New Testament be written directly by an apostle? Explain.

Recommended Reading

Bruce, F. F. *The Canon of Scripture.* Downers Grove, IL: InterVarsity Press, 1988.

Ferguson, Everett. *Backgrounds of Early Christianity.* Grand Rapids: Eerdmans, 2003.

Köstenberger, Andreas J., and Michael J. Kruger. *The Heresy of Orthodoxy: How Contemporary Culture's Fascination with Diversity Has Reshaped Our Understanding of Early Christianity.* Wheaton, IL: Crossway, 2010.

CHAPTER 5

THE EARLIEST CHRISTIANS

In the previous chapters, we looked at the story of the writing of the Old and New Testaments, as well as the process of receiving these books into the Christian canon. We also explored the Septuagint, the Greek translation of the Old Testament.

Along the way, we noted where the story was headed—namely, Christians began to embrace the Apocrypha, while also losing the ability to read Hebrew. The second issue is even more important: once Christians lost the ability to read Hebrew—and also lost regular contact with Jewish Christians—it was easy for some to mistake the Apocrypha as part of the Old Testament. The early centuries do not show this, but over time, we see more people using the Apocrypha, and some beginning to quote it as Scripture.

Another issue surrounding the early church is the question of the New Testament canon. This is more a concern of modern readers, but we frequently hear that the New Testament was in flux for most of the early church. The claim is that the Bible was largely a process of throwing some books out, accepting new books, and ultimately deciding the canon based on power and politics. We will tread lightly, not wading into the dense fog of scholarship on the subject. But we do need a proper understanding of how the Bible was treated in the early church. And how the Bible was treated raises the question of the canon.

The Early Church and the Canon

As we have seen, the Jewish canon was finalized after the Babylonian exile. By the time of the New Testament, Jewish believers were confident in the canon of the Old Testament, though some disputed books like Ruth and Esther. But such debates were over a few books, not the entire canon. If the book of Ruth was debated by some Jews—due to its uncertain origin (though the story itself was not in doubt)—other books were never disputed. In the end, even Ruth was received.

Yet it's one thing to say a few books were disputed, another to say the entire canon was fluctuating and unstable. As with the Old Testament, a few New Testament books were disputed. We know this from Eusebius, a historian of the church from the fourth century. Around AD 325, he wrote his *Ecclesiastical History*, which recounts the early centuries of the church—from the apostles to his day. Eusebius wrote that some books of the New Testament were disputed (*antilegomena*), though he stated they were "recognized by many."[1] The books in question were James, Jude, 2 Peter, and 2 and 3 John. The concern of some, he wrote, was whether these books were really written by James, Jude, Peter, and John. In the end, these books were received as genuine and apostolic.

An analogy may help us to see how the early church came to have disputed books. Let's say we are part of a church in a remote area of the Roman Empire, and it is the early second century. We are a new church and we have in our possession the four Gospels, Paul's letters, 1 John, 1 Peter, and Revelation. After several years, a neighboring church sends a copy of the book of James. The man delivering the book says all churches received this book, and so it should be included in our Scriptures. However, after reading it, we are puzzled by what seems to be the way James rejects Paul's message of faith. The first response of several in the church is that the message of James *might* be contradicting Paul—and besides, who can vouch for the messenger who brought the book to us? Perhaps he is a false Christian or a Roman sent to disrupt us and pollute our message. And so suspicion grows into doubt.

This scenario is a completely hypothetical situation, but it is one that can help us see how disputes might arise. In this case, the dispute would have been invalid, since the church has always understood that James is critiquing a *misreading* of Paul (faith without fruit). But Christians throughout the centuries have, at times, asked the same question of James. Just because there was a dispute does not mean it was a valid dispute, much less that it was a widely held view.

The point is that those in the early church—especially in Christian churches far away from the first apostolic churches—had few resources from which to get quick answers. If doubts—even hard questions—crept in, then a certain amount of doubt might spread throughout a community. It would not take much for doubt to give way to dispute. The fact is, we do not always know why certain books were disputed, and we know some were disputed for poor reasons—like when some Christians later began to doubt the book of Revelation, though Christians had cherished it for a long time.[2]

It can be unsettling to hear that parts of the Bible were disputed. But we must be careful that we do not read *disputed* as a synonym for *rejected* or *despised*. A book may be disputed, but this does not mean it is unloved—and it says nothing about who disputed it, or how many people disputed it. The reason a book is accepted is not because it has universal acclaim but because it bears evidence of divine inspiration, and confidence should not be shaken because someone somewhere raised doubts about a few books.

In fact, if we were to come up with a simple rule for our discussion, there would not be two categories but four:

- Received books—those books universally accepted by the early church.
- Rejected books—books some in the church may have felt were canonical but were later deemed outside the canon (e.g., Maccabees and the Epistle of Barnabas).
- Disputed books—books that are canonical, but some raised doubts about their usage (e.g., Ruth or 2 Peter).
- Heretical books—books embraced by only a few who take issue with orthodox teaching (e.g., the Gospel of Thomas).

This list should help us gain our bearings. Put simply, the issue of certain books being *disputed* should not be cause for alarm, at least not if we understand how scholars use this term. A disputed book should not cause us to lose confidence in the Bible itself.

If these terms are still confusing, we need to grasp one basic idea: the church *assumed* a canon long before they developed the grammar and language to *describe* the canon. The churches had books, and the books of our New Testament were widely shared. The fact that they also asked hard questions at times about certain books should encourage us, because it means they knew that some belonged and others did not.

Indeed, no serious evidence exists of churches approaching their Bibles as a stitched-up collection of their own choosing— some taking three Gospels, others taking new Gospels, and some Christians cheeky enough to try their hand at writing their own books. The important point of our fourfold list of terms is not that some books were disputed, but that nearly all the books of the New Testament were always on the "accepted" list.

The Apocrypha and the Church

But when did the early church begin to use the Apocrypha? We must tread lightly here only because we don't want to complicate things with the debates of scholars (for more, see our recommended reading list). But we can certainly sketch the conclusion. First, all the evidence we have suggests that the early church, including areas with more gentile converts, received the same canon as the Hebrew Bible. The earliest evidence in Christian writings also suggests that the adoption of the Apocrypha was not universal. For example, we know from the Jewish historian Josephus that the structure of the Hebrew Old Testament followed this pattern:

> Among us [the Jews] there are not thousands of books in disagreement and conflict with each other, but only twenty-two books, containing the record of all time, which are rightly trusted.[3]

These twenty-two books are, in fact, the *same* as our Old Testament—though some, like the Minor Prophets, are combined into one book. By combining these books, we arrive at only twenty-two books. This was the canon of the Old Testament by the time of Ezra and Nehemiah—just after the return from exile.

Josephus also notes that the Jews did not close the canon but that it was a result of God's action. The Holy Spirit no longer inspired prophets and writers as he had in the time before the exile—an issue we looked at in chapter 4.

The point here is important. Josephus was a Jewish scholar, and his argument in *Against Apion* has nothing to do with the early Christians. The issue instead was how the Jews approached their Bibles, both in the past and in Josephus's day. This is a good starting place for us, since it allows us to compare the commitment of the Jews according to Josephus and the writings of early Christians. A quick trip through early Christian writings will show that early Christians treated the New Testament with the same view—that it was from God and authenticated by him.

Justin Martyr (AD 100–165) grew up near Jerusalem and, after a life pursuing Greek philosophy, converted to Christianity. Justin is important because he wrote several works that defended Christians— the most important of which for us is *Dialogue with Trypho*, which debated the issues between Jews and Christians. Justin appears to have believed the story of the miraculous writing of the Septuagint (declaring the Greek Bible to be *superior* to the original language, even blaming disparities in the text on the Jews corrupting the Hebrew).

But while he embraced the translation of the Septuagint, Justin never seems to embrace the wider canon of the Apocrypha. None of his sources quote from books outside of the Hebrew canon. It is likely that, while he elevated the Septuagint translation above the Hebrew texts, he nevertheless shared the same view of the canon. At least he does not *use* the Apocrypha in the same way he uses the books of the Old Testament. Theophilus, a contemporary of Justin, also showed no sign of embracing the Apocrypha as part of the Septuagint.

Another important figure is Melito of Sardis (d. 180), who lived in Asia Minor (modern Turkey). Around AD 170, Melito was asked by a friend to list the books of the Old Testament. Melito agreed and offered his rationale as well. He states categorically that he "went East and came to the place where these things were preached and done"—that is to say, he learned the order of the Old Testament from those who lived closer to Jerusalem. Echoing New Testament (and Jewish) language, Melito referred to the Old Testament as the *Law and Prophets*. His list included the five books of Moses, fourteen others (including historical and poetical books), then six books of Prophets (including Ezra-Nehemiah), but does not include Tobit, Judith, Maccabees, Wisdom, Sirach, etc. It contains twenty-five books. If Kings, Samuel, and Chronicles were counted as three books instead of six, and if Ruth was joined to Judges, then there would be twenty-one. The only omission is Esther—which, if added, would bring the number to twenty-two, or the same canonical list as Josephus.

The evidence—and there is more we could share—suggests there was no widespread use of the Apocrypha as Scripture in the earliest centuries of the church. Indeed, one of the more notable comments is found in the *Exhortation to the Greeks*, probably written in the third century. Unhappy with the claim that Christians followed their own understanding of the Old Testament, the author fired back that "the books relating to our religion are to this day preserved among the Jews." He wrote that no one wished to create a stand-alone Christian canon since "we demand that they be produced from the synagogue of the Jews."[4] Such language is rather striking for its later date. The relationship between Christians and Jews was increasingly strained by the third century—though not yet to the point of open hostility—yet the Christian witness remained firm that the Old Testament was received from the Jewish canon.

We could go on, but this proves the basic point. Because early Christians relied on the Septuagint for their Old Testament canon does not mean they quickly embraced the extra books of the Apocrypha in the Septuagint. Those who were aware of the differences in the Hebrew and Greek Old Testaments often resolved the tension by adopting the Jewish canon, not the additional books found in the Septuagint—and in the case of *Exhortation to the Greeks*, some Christians even demanded that churches base their Bibles on the pattern found in synagogues.

Of course, early Christians did eventually embrace the Apocrypha as part of the Old Testament. By the fourth century, during his work on the Vulgate, Jerome assumed at first that even the Jews viewed the Apocrypha as canonical. He was shocked to learn the truth. We will look at the Vulgate in our next chapter, but we need to understand what happened between the second and fourth centuries. The early evidence shows a conventional approach, like that of the Jews, that saw only the twenty-two books of Josephus as the canonical books of the Old Testament.

In terms of when Christians began to adopt the Apocrypha, there is no smoking gun. No single individual foisted the Apocrypha on others. What seems most likely is that the church over time lost touch with the early approach. The Apocrypha remained alongside the Old Testament, and so these books grew in stature. This is not uncommon in the history of the Bible—things placed alongside the text, at times, came to be seen as authoritative. This fact would be an even stronger draw for Christians, since the Apocrypha were written in a style similar to other books of the Old Testament. In short, it does not seem to have been an intentional, malicious choice for the Apocrypha to grow increasingly in the minds of Christians—to the point that these books became joined to the Bible. Today, Eastern Orthodox and Roman Catholic churches continue to hold the Apocrypha as inspired and part of their Bibles. It was not until the Reformation, with the recovery of the study of Hebrew, that Protestants began to remove these books from their Bibles.

The New Testament Canon

By this point, we could describe the early church as a people committed to the received books of the Hebrew Bible. What is striking about this fact is that these same early Christians are today sometimes accused of approaching the New Testament canon with disinterest. Scholars, books, articles, blogs—not a few today assume that no fixed canon of the New Testament was in place until centuries *after* the first century. In other words, the claim is that the canon of the New Testament was fluid. Different versions of the Gospels, for example, are said to be everywhere, with the Bible not being fully in place until perhaps the Council of Nicaea in 325.[5]

This is not how we ought to read the evidence. It is true that the first-century church did not populate lists of which books were to be received in the canon. Nor did they clarify in writing how they received the Old Testament. We must not mistake the lack of evidence as meaning they had no opinion on the subject.

Perhaps a good starting point is to realize the clear difference between an *idea* and the *defense* of an idea. This is something we experience every day—we know something is true though we have never been asked to give an explicit reason why. For example, one of us teaches theology and assigns students to write out their theological confessions. Nearly all the students chuckle when they get to an important belief only to realize they have never written their view, in detail, along with a defense of their belief. One can believe something without doing apologetics.

The canon in the early church functioned the same way. The early church had a consistent belief that New Testament books were to be treated as Scripture. They disputed only a very few books that some had doubts about, but they never felt pressured to provide works that defended this position. Again, the fact that certain books would be disputed at all shows that the early church knew that only inspired books belong in the New Testament. However, as time wore on—and as some began to challenge received books—the church began to defend its position. But even then, the assumption was always that the canon is something *received*, not something they *created*.

One of the more scandalous figures to attempt such a challenge was Marcion (AD 85–160), a preacher's kid from the region of modern Turkey along the Black Sea. A number of factors—personal and theological—seem to have driven Marcion to hate the Jewish origins of the faith. It is at least probable that he did not like Jews in his own community, and the notorious revolt led by Simon bar Kokhba in AD 132 also may have triggered Marcion. No matter the cause, the conclusion Marcion reached was that the Jewish origins of the church needed to be trimmed.

Marcion meant this literally. He tossed out the entire Old Testament—he even claimed the God of the Old Testament was all wrath and fury and must be cast off for the New Testament God of grace and mercy. He then tossed out the majority of the New Testament, unable to escape most of its Jewish origins. In the end, all Marcion had left was the Gospel of Luke (which he pared back) and the letters of Paul (but only Romans through 2

Thessalonians). At least it would have been a small Bible, easy to carry!

Partly in response to Marcion, the church began to clarify which New Testament books it accepted as canonical. Around AD 240 Origen mentioned the twenty-seven New Testament books by name, which he called "trumpets hammered thin," a charming image of a loud anthem played on the thin pages of the Bible. Seventy years later, Eusebius—the church historian we mentioned—discussed several disputes over the canonicity of James, Jude, 2 Peter, and 2 and 3 John. But what many forget is that, while Eusebius says these books are disputed, he affirms they are "nevertheless known to most," meaning most churches accepted them as inspired. He even says James and Jude were read in most churches. So we must not see the term *disputed text* as a sign that the church did not accept them almost everywhere. From the beginning, the church had a concept of books that must be received because of apostolic authority, so the fact that some Christians were uncertain is not to say every book was on the chopping block. The need to clarify the canon, explaining why some books were received, was not a sudden impulse to create a Bible from scratch.

There was a benefit to the disputes, since they matured the way Christians reflected on the subject of biblical authority. The *Muratorian Fragment*—named for the man who discovered it in the eighteenth century—has one such list that is meant to clarify the received Bible and to refute two counterfeit Pauline letters forged to support Marcion's view. The text is not perfect, since it is only a fragment and a horrible translation into Latin. But what we have reveals a list that is quite close to our New Testament, failing to mention a few of the later epistles like 1 Peter and James. None of these texts were said to be rejected books of the New Testament.[6] Almost two centuries later, Athanasius wrote a customary Easter Letter as bishop of Alexandria, in whch he took up the subject of the New Testament canon. By this stage, however, the process had matured fully and Athanasius could list each of the twenty-seven books of the New Testament as being canonized.

There is more evidence, and there is more to discuss about the New Testament canon. All biblical scholars are aware that some books were disputed, but despite claims of widespread confusion about the Bible, the evidence suggests that complaints were relatively few. No one describes one of the Gospels or a letter of Paul as being disputed. Even for those books that were disputed, the problems were uncommon and often local problems within individual churches. The early church received nearly all the books of our New Testament without controversy. Several books were disputed, but even then, most of them were embraced as written by an apostle. This should dispel notions that the church had a fluid list of books in the New Testament. Some certainly rejected the canon and thus left the church—as Marcion did. But the clear belief of early Christians was that the canon was something *received*, not something they *created*.

Study Questions

1. Do you find it troubling that certain books of the New Testament were disputed?

2. Have you read any books of the Apocrypha? If so, what was your impression of them?

3. Because books like those in the Apocrypha were confused as Scripture, do you think we should take

caution when including things in our Bibles (notes, confessions, other texts)? Why or why not?

Recommended Reading

Carson, D. A., ed. *The Enduring Authority of Christian Scriptures.* Wheaton, IL: Crossway, 2016.

Hill, Charles. *Who Chose the Gospels?* Oxford: Oxford University Press, 2012.

Kruger, Michael. *Canon Revisited: Establishing the Origins and Authority of the New Testament Books.* Wheaton, IL: Crossway, 2012.

CHAPTER 6

THE VULGATE

The Catholic translation still normative for today is known as the Latin Vulgate. It is a translation both admired and scorned—used by Catholic churches in the West for centuries, rejected by Protestants as an inferior translation of the original languages. In fact, the love and hate for the Vulgate were products of the Reformation. Used by Christians for almost a thousand years, the Vulgate became an object of Reformation critique of the medieval church, a Bible locked away from the people, unintelligible to them. In response, the Catholic Church stressed the beauty and historic origins of their Bible, even condemning use of any translation except the Vulgate. So committed was the Catholic Church to this translation, in fact, that these rules were relaxed only in the twentieth century at the Second Vatican Council.

The origin of the Vulgate, though, is far more interesting than these later fights suggest. For starters, we must recognize the Vulgate's role for Christians in the West. Over the course of its history, the Vulgate influenced the shape of liturgy, the interpretation of passages, and the struggle to define Protestants and Catholics. It was translated in the fourth century by Jerome, a man who, when he finished the text, was known as one of the most learned men of his generation in biblical studies. Indeed, until the start of modern biblical research, few would surpass him.

But the Vulgate did not secure its place in Western history easily. As we shall see, it was not well received in Jerome's lifetime—or for centuries after his death. It was seen by many as a newfangled translation, disrespectful to the Septuagint. Only after this initially poor reception did the Western church take the Vulgate into its bosom.

Jerome

The man who translated the Vulgate was known by contemporaries as a gracious friend and a bitter enemy. At times people found him to be a great big grump. Cross him, and he was often blunt and capable of scorching words—and not even his friends were thrilled with his candor. But to history, Jerome was a man of great learning who established anew the Bible for the West.[1]

Jerome was born in AD 347 in what was then Dalmatia and Pannonia. (In Jerome's day, this was considered part of northern Italy.) His family was Christian, and he was raised in the church, though we know little about his upbringing. We know his family was wealthy, and this lifestyle provoked in Jerome a desire for intellectual distinction. Latin was probably not his native language. He probably spoke Greek or maybe Illyrian, an Indo-European language that is lost today. Jerome wanted to gain culture and education, and by his teenage years he had made his way to one of the epicenters of antiquity, the city of Rome. In Rome, Jerome came to master Latin and to gain sophistication in rhetoric and the classical disciplines of the ancient intellectual world. In Rome he found a rich marketplace of ideas and teachers—just the sort of education he craved.

Jerome was distinguished too by the fame of his Latin teacher,

Aelius Donatus. Donatus was a capable teacher who would become the most famous Latin grammarian in Western history. He wrote a Latin grammar book—the *Ars grammatica*—that would be used so widely in the Middle Ages that subsequent basic textbooks on any subject were named after him (*donet*). Indeed, there could have been some argument that the first book printed on the new Gutenberg press should be Donatus's book.[2] For Jerome, Donatus was a faithful tutor, who taught him not only to know Latin but to understand the polished speech that comes from the study of rhetoric. A man who studied rhetoric would be like someone who studied law or medicine today—both respectable and potentially lucrative professions. Jerome was grabbing for the brass ring.

Before he reached the age of thirty, however, the luster of intellectual life began to fade. We know little of these years, but we know that Jerome was not entirely without faith. He was baptized shortly after arriving in Rome, and he tells us later how he wandered the catacombs, viewing the relics of the martyrs, dreading the thought of damnation. Perhaps his baptism was inspired by a searching for fulfillment, but if he expected baptism to instantly change him, he nevertheless remained the same career-driven man who had come to Rome. The classics remained his focus. Like his contemporary, Augustine of Hippo, Jerome found living a life of pleasure more enjoyable than practicing his relatively new faith.

Jerome only found dedication to the Christian life in the face of serious illness. Traveling through modern Bulgaria and Turkey (ancient Thrace and Asia Minor), Jerome was struck down with a serious illness. He wrote, "Preparations were made for my funeral. My whole body grew cold, and life's vital warmth only lingered faintly in my poor throbbing breast."[3]

Two of Jerome's friends were also struck down and eventually died. Infirm and dreading the end of his earthly life, Jerome saw a vision that ordered him to lay aside his secular pursuits and take up a life of Christian asceticism. Jerome recovered and set out immediately, not to Rome, but to the desert. The laurels of intellectual fame he exchanged for the rag-and-bone life of a hermit.[4]

Jerome made an honest attempt at the hermetical life—meaning he attempted to become a solitary hermit, living in the desert, devoted to a life of prayer. He would never become a serious enough monk, however, to abandon all of life's pursuits. Rather he found that his talent for study was a tool he could use to study the Bible. He traveled to Palestine and surrounding areas, where he continued his study of Greek and began to take an interest in Hebrew. In the end, he abandoned hope of becoming a perpetual desert father and retreated instead to Antioch.

The study of Hebrew would be the most important tool Jerome gained during this phase of life—one he would continue to hone for the rest of his career. Those who wanted to learn Hebrew had a steep road to climb, since knowledge of Hebrew was not acquired easily. Hebrew teachers were hard to come by. At times, we see an indirect form of anti-Jewish rhetoric too, as many would suggest the Hebrew text was not only irrelevant but harmful in the life of Christians. Even for those who wanted to learn Hebrew, it was not as widespread as Greek and Latin, and those who knew Greek could always study the Septuagint. To help himself learn Hebrew, Jerome sought the help of a converted Jew, and he soon found the language of the Old Testament to be deeply satisfying as it continued to nurture his mind while also rousing his faith.

Jerome traveled next to Constantinople—which had become the heart of the Roman Empire since its founding by Constantine in the early AD 300s. He worked with Gregory Nazianzus, who was one of the most important theologians of the generation. Nazianzus would play a role at the Council of Constantinople, which gave final shape to the Nicene Creed as we know it today.[5] From there, Jerome traveled back to the West, where he was ordained to the priesthood—against his will, according to tradition, and only with the stipulation he would be allowed to remain a hermit. By the early AD 380s, Jerome was settled for a season as the secretary to Pope Damasus I.

Jerome's role as secretary was not merely functionary. These were grim days for the church. It had achieved by this time a measure of victory over Arianism—the belief that only the Father is fully God, while the Son and Spirit were either created or subordinate. But other problems were still spawning—namely, the teachings of Apollinarism and the Pneumatomachi. These views were identified as heresies, meaning they promoted teachings that were proved to be contrary to the meaning of the Bible. But even with these new movements on the rise, Arianism was the most important debate in the early church. The basic principle of Arianism is that the Son in his divine nature is a creature—certainly exalted above humans or angels, but essentially a creature and not fully God.

The original Nicene Creed had stressed, against the teachings of Arius, that the Son was "the same essence" (*homoousias*) as the Father.[6] He was not *created* at a moment in time, nor was he *subordinate* throughout eternity to the Father; all the same qualities the Bible uses to describe the Father are said also of the Son. Both are eternal, to be worshiped, and able to forgive sins. Therefore, it would be contrary to the Bible to speak of a hierarchy within God (Father over Son) or of the Son as a creature (making him closer to humans than to the Father). But the Nicene Creed covered only this central issue; it was not a full statement about the triune

God. As a result, other problems were always possible—and the Arian instinct to divide the persons of the Trinity could always be affirmed in slightly different terms. This is how the Pneumato-machi ("combaters against the Spirit") arose, who seemed to grant that the Son was equal with the Father, yet carried on the logic of Arianism by denying the Holy Spirit was fully God.

Apollinarism was more a problem of over-applying the cure against Arianism than a continuation of earlier heresies. Admit-ting that the Son is fully God, it began to question how the Son, as God, could be incarnate in human flesh. Understanding how a creature or an angel could take on human flesh was not the issue, but once the Son was properly understood as fully God, the mystery of the incarnation became more capable of leading some into error.

The teaching came, as the name suggests, from Appollinaris. He recoiled from Arianism and fully embraced the Nicene faith. Jesus was fully God, come down to save. Still, Appollinaris made the mistake of stressing the divine nature of the Son so much that he gave less attention to the equally biblical teaching that the Son "tabernacled [dwelled] among us" in human flesh (John 1:14). Appollinaris assumed the incarnation needed to be located some-where in the person of Jesus; it needed an entry point. This entry point, he decided, was in the mind of Jesus—with him having a human body and soul but only a divine mind. The result of this teaching was that Jesus was not like us in every way ("fully human in every way," Hebrews 2:17) but instead only mostly human.

Both issues took up the bulk of Jerome's work under Pope Damasus. Synods and councils were called throughout the Roman Empire, all hoping to end these problems. As the secretary to Damasus, and as a trusted scholar in biblical studies, Jerome was asked to write his answers on theological matters. And while it would have been understandable if Jerome had devoted himself to the defense of orthodoxy, a greater need was pressing on the West: the need for a better translation of the Bible into Latin. Indeed, the need for the Scriptures for the West was seen, in part, as the solution to the issue of heresy. Translation work always requires a careful and scholarly mind—skills that must be earned through years of hard work. The translator (or team of translators) needs not only financial support but church support as well, or else the translation would not be valued or used in churches.

The need was not felt for centuries since both Old and New Testaments were already in Greek. The Western half of the church, however, grew increasingly reliant on Latin as the common language. Over the first centuries of the church, there was not yet a complete translation of the Bible into Latin. Some early attempts were poor attempts to render the text into Old Latin. More on these problems in a moment.

But the translation came about in fact at the suggestion of Pope Damasus, who was himself from Spain and would have been aware of the problem of bad translations into Old Latin. We know Damasus first ordered Jerome to translate the Gospels, and Jerome's later preface to the Gospels gives us a number of details about the project. The work began sometime in AD 382, though it hit a snag within two years, as Damasus passed away in AD 384. As it turns out, this apparent setback was the catalyst that led Jerome to expand his work beyond merely a translation of the Gospels. With the pope gone, he was freed of his administrative obligations to Rome, but he was also freed to go beyond Damasus's initial dream of translating only the Gospels to translate the entire Bible.

Within two years, Jerome settled in Bethlehem, where he would spend roughly thirty years on the Vulgate translation. There he would again take up the study of Hebrew—a unique part of his story, as he now became fluent in the language. But his journey to translate the Bible would also become a journey to the canonical sources, especially the Jewish sources, of the text he was translating.

Latin Bibles: Old and New

Why was there a need for a new Latin translation? As we have already said, despite modern assumptions, the Vulgate was not the first translation of the Bible into Latin.

By Jerome's day, the Latin language was ancient, though used entirely in the West. Julius Caesar was born a century before the birth of Christ, and when he learned to speak Latin, the language was already centuries old. Prior to the time of Christ, in fact, the spread of the Roman Republic (begun roughly in the sixth-century BC) had made the use of Latin a requirement if subjugated people wished to speak to their new masters. Those in the East balked at this, but the spread of Latin in Western regions was crucial. The wide use of the language was due to the might of Rome. It was a prestige language, learned as a second language by those who wished to engage the Western world.

One feature of Latin was that it evolved rapidly. Those of us who study Latin today learn *classical Latin*—the eloquent Latin of men like Cicero and Livy. But that classical phase of Latin began only around the time of Caesar and Christ.

To understand the importance of the Vulgate, we first should realize that Latin was an established language, though the church had for centuries been largely Greek speaking. By the early fourth century, nearly all the major works of theology were written in

Greek, not Latin. The expansion of the faith into Europe, however, created a need for a translation for non-Greek-speaking Christians, and Latin was the most accessible language. Unfortunately, the early Latin translations were often poor attempts to translate the Bible.

So, by the time of Jerome, there were several versions of the Bible in Latin. These versions are known today as the "Old Latin" versions (*Vetus Latina*). This can be confusing because *Old Latin*, strictly speaking, is the much older form of Latin derived from the Etruscans. The Old Latin *language* is somewhat like the difference between modern English and the Middle English of Geoffrey Chaucer (which is all but gibberish to those untrained in it). These Old Latin translations, then, were not using this ancient Latin. What makes these early Latin Bibles "old" is that they are older than Jerome's Vulgate. Making things more confusing is that the phrase "Old Latin Bible" does not refer to a single translation but to a wide variety of texts—some of which are mentioned only when Latin theologians cite the Bible in their works. All we need to understand is that there were rough translations into Latin before the time of Jerome.

The quality of these translations was awful, and their style and fidelity to the Greek of the Septuagint and New Testament were often sloppy. These texts did not use the original Hebrew, so those portions of the Old Testament would have been a translation of a translation. Even if these texts had been faithful to the original languages, the style of the Latin was, at times, stiff and lifeless.

This again raises the point of whether a translation should follow a word-for-word method or find a dynamic equivalent. For example, a figure of speech in one language rarely means the same thing in another language—thus ruining the value of translating word for word, since the meaning is lost on readers. You can imagine, for example, someone translating the English idiom "*hold your horses*" word for word into another language—and the head-scratching that would result. Of course, sometimes idioms and expressions are carried over, and they *do* stick in the new language—as Isaiah 40:15 gave English speakers the phrase "*a drop in a bucket*." But the risk is always high that the translation will create confusion.

The Old Latin translations were often word for word, yet still managed to cause confusion. Sometimes the words were translated as if someone simply looked up each word and wrote the Latin equivalent. Some were more polished, but these texts as a whole were unhelpful for Christians.

The surviving texts we have in Old Latin (such as the *Vercelli Codex* in Verona) were written in a variety of styles, but they most often use only capital letters without spaces, punctuation, or division. There were several reasons for this, the most important the economy of space, since writing materials were expensive. Many ancient languages would do this, including Greek. But the risk of confusion is obvious: words run together or can be confused.

The situation with the Old Latin translations was pitiful—but we should add that the pitiful state was not due to a lack of desire to give the Bible to Christians. These copies were almost always intended for worship or small group settings. Though imperfect, the texts were not the result of moral corruption. The problems were due to the rot of history, the creep of language, since bad copies were used to make other copies. By the fourth century, not a single edition could be used as a standard. Jerome wrote in his preface to the Vulgate that each Old Latin copy he found differed from the next.

The "Radical" Vulgate

The primary issue with the Old Latin versions was their source material. To make the point again: by the time the Bible began to appear in Latin, the church had come to rely heavily on the Greek translation of the Old Testament, the Septuagint. When Jerome began his translation, he had no firsthand knowledge of the origins of the Septuagint. The poor quality of the Old Latin translations sparked in his mind the desire to find older texts of the biblical books. He did not feel comfortable with simply editing the existing Latin copies.

One of the works he consulted was the *Hexapla*, a third-century compendium made by the theologian Origen (c. AD 185–c. 254). No copy survives today, but we know how the conpendium worked. If someone turned to the book of Genesis, for example, each page was broken into columns: one in Hebrew, the next a transliteration of the Hebrew into Greek.[7] There were then four Greek translations of the Hebrew. For someone like Jerome, this was a bolt from the blue. The ability to compare texts, most of which were older than even Origen's, gave Jerome a path to ask questions, not only of the Latin translations of his day but also of the Septuagint itself.

For example, we know that Jerome around this time altered his translation of Psalms. Pope Damasus had asked for the Gospels, but Jerome was perhaps personally inspired to include Psalms. The first edition he made is known today as the *Roman Psalter*—named for its origin when Jerome worked in Rome. This edition became popular in medieval Rome but almost nowhere else. After his work in the Hexapla, however, Jerome produced a revised edition known as the *Gallican Psalter*—named for its popularity in northern Europe (*Gaul*). This edition was similar to the Roman edition, but Jerome had now checked the Latin against the various Greek translations and made improvements.

Perhaps this was the cause of greater ideas in Jerome's mind. Having to repeat work on the Psalms due to shoddy manuscripts, Jerome felt chastened. Since the texts he was using were not ideal, was he not grasping at straws if he continued to use them?

At some point around AD 390, Jerome abandoned his reliance on the Greek versions in the *Hexapla* and settled in Bethlehem, close to Jewish scholars who could train him. Jerome again plunged into the study of Hebrew. He befriended a man who, for fear of upsetting his Jewish neighbors, agreed to teach him in secret. For nearly fifteen years, Jerome was a devoted student of the language of the Israelites.

As often happens, too much zeal for biblical languages began to concern Jerome's neighbors. Other Christians were alarmed when Jerome declared that the books of the Apocrypha were not part of the Bible, that they had never been used by the Jews as Scripture, and that Christians had errantly included them in their Bibles because of the Septuagint. Jerome nowNot abandoned the translation of the Apocrypha. He had already translated the books of Judith and Tobit, but he tossed them out and never translated any other books of the Apocrypha. It is one of history's ironies that the man who translated the Vulgate—a book today synonymous with Catholic acceptance of the Apocrypha—never translated these books. The copies of the Apocrypha found today in the Vulgate, in fact, are edited versions of the Old Latin texts, not translations from Jerome.

The Vulgate and the Middle Ages

Jerome was a man committed to original texts and original languages. We are unsure which Hebrew texts he used, and many have wished to peer over his shoulder while he worked. We should also admit that later scholars will find his translation uneven. He did all his work alone, so perhaps we can overlook its flaws. In most of his translation, he focused on the Hebrew and Greek meaning without first adjusting it to fit classical Latin. In other words, Jerome's method was typically a word-for-word approach.

Although we can dispute the quality of the work, we should not question his motivation, his candor about what he discovered in his studies, or his commitment to translating the Bible to the highest standards possible. By the standards of his day, Jerome produced a marvelous translation almost single-handedly for a Latin-speaking West that needed the Bible.

We cannot finish the story of the Vulgate without saying something of its later history. At some point during Jerome's work on the translation, it became evident that some Catholics were unhappy with Jerome's claims about the Apocrypha. Augustine offered a mixed opinion, for example, accepting Jerome's opinion (the Apocrypha is not canon) but rejecting his conclusion (it should be removed). On two occasions in his works,[8] Augustine took up the question, the most important of which is his earlier work *On Christian Doctrine*—a work about the study of theology and the Bible. He instructed his readers to focus, if necessary, only on those books that are canonical, though he wanted to allow Christians to read the Apocrypha, since those books were important in the history of Israel. A few Protestant denominations would later take this same tactic—especially the Lutherans, who consider the Apocrypha to be *deuterocanonical* (of a lesser authority).

The clearest evidence of unhappiness with Jerome's translation came from those who refused to actually *use* it. For centuries after Jerome's death in AD 420, very few churches adopted the

Vulgate. This judgment is based on the fact that there are few surviving copies from the centuries immediately after Jerome. This implies that few were made, thus few survived. For example, we have only 110 pages (or leaves) of a Vulgate copy from the fifth century (housed today in St. Gall, Switzerland).[9] By contrast, we have scores of Bibles (or fragments of Bibles) from the same period in the Old Latin tradition. Scribes continued to copy their old standard texts.

The church clung to its beloved Old Latin translations even if the language in them was archaic. This is ironic, as the Vulgate would undergo the same process when it was held aloft at the Council of Trent in the 1500s as the only translation for Catholics, long after the Latin language was all but dead. The same could be said for Protestants in the last century who clung doggedly to their King James Version. This type of tension between long-*established* versions of the Bible and a new version based on original texts is a common feature in the story of the Bible.

In Jerome's day, these problems cast enough doubt on the Vulgate that it took centuries for it to be received in the Catholic Church.

Study Questions

1. Why did Pope Damasus call for a new Latin translation?
2. Was it a good thing to have the Bible in Latin? Explain.
3. What did Jerome discover when he began to study biblical languages?
4. Why do you think Christians cling to specific translations of the Bible? Is this wrong?

Recommended Reading

De Hamel, Christopher. *The Book: A History of the Bible*. London: Phaidon, 2001.

Van Liere, Frans. *An Introduction to the Medieval Bible*. Cambridge: Cambridge University Press, 2014.

CHAPTER 7

THE MEDIEVAL BIBLE

British English and American English have different spellings for the same words. For example, the British English of words *honour, colour,* and *programme* are changed in American English to *honor, color,* and *program.*

What is not often known is that these differences come largely from the work of one man: Noah Webster (1758–1853). A scholar and a fierce nationalist for America, Webster pushed to create unique traits in English that would match the separation of America from its homeland. The publication in 1806 of his *A Compendious Dictionary of the English Language* was based not solely on a desire to provide a dictionary for Americans but also on his desire to rid Americans of their ties to England. His nemesis was Samuel Johnson, who had published a dictionary in England in 1755. But, as Webster knew, the creation of a standard language would create a unified culture. One language, taught to everyone, would grow a young nation into a shared identity.

This same process of standardization occurred with the use of Latin in the medieval period. Just as the Latin language stopped being used in Europe, the Carolingian Renaissance threw down the gauntlet against those who abandoned Latin. This renaissance was a movement funded by Charlemagne and his successors in the eighth century. One of their main goals was to *formalize* the

91

use of Latin among scholars and churchmen. Carolingian scholars also championed a newer, polished version of the Vulgate—and by doing so, established it as the quintessential medieval Bible.

The Long Acceptance of the Vulgate

As we saw in the previous chapter, the Vulgate was marginalized in Western churches for at least several centuries after the death of Jerome. The Vulgate was based on Jerome's increasing commitment to the original languages, especially to the Hebrew canon. But since he removed the Apocrypha, early medieval Christians had qualms about adopting the Vulgate in their churches. Jerome also lacked official sanction for his Bible, since Pope Damasus had commissioned only an updated version of the Gospels based on the well-known Greek New Testament. One scholar has noted that in copies of the Vulgate, later scribes began to reintroduce portions of the Apocrypha that Jerome trimmed from the Bible.[1] The Old Latin version was not going down without a fight.

The adoption of the Vulgate across the West involved several men who championed it, two in particular who are worth noting. The first was the Venerable Bede (ca. 672–735), known to students of medieval history for his detailed description of the Anglo-Saxons. But he was equally important in the development of theological writing in the northern part of Europe. Bede carried back to Northumbria (in modern Britain) a copy of the Vulgate that likely inspired later copies of it in both England and Ireland.[2] A small influence it may seem, but the spread of any translation before the advent of modern marketing and electronic media often required this type of personal connection. Bede did not bring just any Bible; he brought the Vulgate. And that text was copied again and again, further spreading its influence.

The second champion of the Vulgate—indirectly, at least—was Charlemagne (AD 741–814). The most well-known of the Frankish kings, Charlemagne helped reestablish what would become the Holy Roman Empire—a kingdom that would exist until Napoleon deposed the last emperor in 1806. In the ninth century, however, Charlemagne needed to galvanize the European lands he had taken in war. To achieve this, he began to recruit and fund the greatest intellectuals in the West to his court in Aachen (in modern Germany), where they established a library specially equipped to produce copies of the Bible.

In a sense, the collecting of scholars was natural for a king (modern governments still fund research and the arts). But what Charlemagne did—perhaps without realizing it—was create a base of influence that would shape the future of Europe. The palace at Aachen became famous, as scholars wished to go there and mingle with their peers. Those who visited Charlemagne's court glimpsed a spectacle that is hard to describe, with everything from a Roman bath to a small zoo (*menagerie*) that housed an elephant, lions, monkeys, and exotic birds. Once done exploring these curiosities, the visitor could then go the scriptorium, where he would see the production of written materials firsthand.

Over time, the *Carolingian Renaissance* managed to revive the intellectual world of Europe, allowing it to take a slow march out of the Dark Ages, when scholarship had been somewhat rare. Historians lament the centuries before Charlemagne for all that was lost, especially those gaps in our knowledge of the early Middle Ages. Charlemagne envisioned a return to former glory—and to achieve this, he leveraged the memory of the great minds of the ancient world of Greece and Rome. If he could re-create but a portion of that old vitality, lost when Rome collapsed in the West, then Charlemagne would be content.

Not surprisingly, an impressive number of written materials flew from Aachen to the corners of Europe—regulations for church and state, official documents, copies of famous scholarly works, and copies of the Bible. Many of these texts came as part and parcel of the function of government, though from the start they included religious edicts about worship, holidays, and even the copying of the Bible.

One of the most important figures, personally recruited by Charlemagne, was Alcuin (AD 735–804). Having served as a teacher at the cathedral of York in northern England, he met Charlemagne in 781. The emperor was impressed and invited him to Aachen to supervise the resurgence that Charlemagne desired. Alcuin was to be the tip of the spear—overseeing not only the expansion of bishops and churches throughout the empire, but also the copying of Bibles for each of these new churches.

Latin was the language of choice, but the work of Alcuin supported what would prove to be a language on the decline. By the ninth century, Latin was already on its downward slope in Europe, as the European languages we know today were beginning to emerge. Latin was still used by intellectuals—especially those from a variety of countries who needed a common language to communicate. Thus, when the Vulgate Bible became the standard text used by Alcuin, who wished to champion only the Latin Bible, Alcuin was in fact reinforcing a dying language as the standard for the Bible. One wonders if Alcuin truly understood that Latin would never again be spoken as it was in the classical age of Rome.

Charlemagne issued an edict in AD 789 calling for reform of Latin manuscripts (as well as Christian liturgies). By issuing this command, Charlemagne launched scholars at Aachen into a fever of intellectual work, mostly around the preservation of ancient books and the correction of bad Latin to conform to classic Latin from the age of Cicero. The work was expanded to cities like Tours, in modern France, and to other smaller workshops, all eager to get involved with Charlemagne's reforms. The influence of Charlemagne and Alcuin cannot be overstated. It was in Aachen where the word *Bible* (*bibliotheca*) became the word of choice to refer to the Scriptures.

A final note on the changes to the Bible at Aachen. In the effort to reform the Latin copies of the Bible, the Carolingian Renaissance created a new style of handwriting that would forever change the West. The script is known as *"Carolingian minuscule"* and used rounded letters, spaces between words, and line breaks—all features we still use today. The result was a form of handwriting that made the text easier to read—and more natural to copy. The purpose of developing this handwriting was to lower the chance of errors by the copyist (a problem for most of history until the printing press). In later centuries, use of the *Gothic Blackletter* style became widespread—seen even today during the Christmas season in phrases like *Ye Olde Shoppe*. Humanist print shops would later develop this same script in their printing, thereby linking the Carolingian script to later forms of modern writing. So as we practice our handwriting as children, we are unknowingly connected to Charlemagne, Alcuin, and the Latin Vulgate.

The invention of Carolingian minuscule partially explains the increased use of the Vulgate. Put simply, the scribes at Aachen were creating a better Bible—more useful for scholars, easier to read for priests, and funded by the Roman Empire. The issue for the medieval church was not only the cost (which they could not control) but the quality of the work. A better Bible meant that churches came to love the new Vulgate.

Big Bibles, Little Bibles, Important Bibles

A few things can be said about the evolving shape of the Bible. Nearly all of us, when we purchase a physical copy of the Bible, end up with the same book in our hands: a single volume, bound at the spine, with onionskin pages. The font, ink, and other features and materials used in the production of modern Bibles are almost always the same (or at least similar in style). This was not the case in the medieval period.

First, the Bible often needed to be copied into several volumes. It is actually quite rare to find a medieval Bible in a single volume. There were several formats that became popular in medieval copies of the Bible. One of the most common was the *Octateuch*—an expansion of the Pentateuch to include the books up to Ruth. The four Gospels were often copied as one, likely because it made for easier use in worship when read aloud before the sermon. Other combinations make sense according to their genre or author. For example, the letters of Paul might be copied into a single volume.

The result is that various volumes take on different roles in worship or study. For example, in medieval worship, the practice arose of bringing the Gospels into the midst of the people to be read, a practice not done for other volumes.

The other feature of medieval Bibles was how they grew and shrunk between AD 600 and 1400. One of the more humorous developments was the popularity of the large size of some Bibles, especially after the reign of Charlemagne. Perhaps the Bible grew in size as a sign of status, but it may have been an issue of convenience, as larger pages could accommodate more text—or at least more space between words and sentences. The most outrageous example of this trend is the infamous *Giant Bible* (*Codex Gigas*), housed today in the National Library of Stockholm. Also known as the Devil's Bible for a lurid, full-page illustration of the devil in the book of Revelation, it was created at a monastery in Bohemia, now the Czech Republic. A solitary monk copied the Bible all by himself, and his sanity has been doubted ever since. At least, there is no explaining this beast of a Bible. It is 36 inches tall, almost 9 inches thick, and weighs 165 pounds. One has trouble imagining how such a book could ever be used—or if its only purpose was to make the biggest Bible in human history. If so, the monk succeeded.

Yet we do not imply that all medieval Bibles were strange. Many of the ornate copies made in the medieval period qualify as works of art. Given the expense of each page created, the execution of large illustrations—some a full page in length—along with the intricate calligraphic art featuring the initial letter of a page is simply astonishing.

For some scholars, the most interesting surviving texts are from *before* the medieval period—three full editions of the Bible in Greek. They are each known by the name "codex," meaning a bound book with a spine like we have today. The second part of their name tells us where they were discovered or housed. They are the *Codex Vaticanus*, the *Codex Alexandrinus*, and the *Codex Sinaiticus*. The first, of course, is located today in the Vatican; the others were discovered in Egypt and the Sinai Peninsula. Scholars have theories about where these copies may have been created, but they don't know for certain. They are valuable tools in modern research.

The Cost of Bibles

The most critical challenge in the Middle Ages was the cost of producing a Bible. It is difficult to overstate the problem. For example, Bible copies made at Jarrow (in northern England) are some of the most famous from the early medieval period. Among them, the most famous is the *Codex Amiatinus*, the oldest complete edition of the Vulgate to survive and direct inspiration for the equally famous *Lindisfarne Gospels*.

These copies were wildly expensive. Each required roughly fifteen-hundred sheep to produce enough hides—later turned into parchment—to make one complete Bible (in three volumes).[3] The *Leon Bible* (AD 960) was created in modern Spain, and it took an estimated 155 cows to produce. While these were agrarian days and animals were plentiful in some areas, the sheer number of animal skins needed to produce one copy of the Bible is staggering. And this is not even factoring in the cost of manufacturing ink, quills, and binding for the final books. To top it off, there needed to be at least one scribe with a practiced hand, capable of copying the text. Ideally, several scribes would work in unison— but then a supervisor was needed to ensure each page passed without errors. A well-stocked and well-trained monastery would typically produce two to four complete Bibles annually. Even this speed was not always possible. A monk working in what is modern Brussels indicated that, while he wanted to make a complete copy of the Bible every two years, it sometimes took him a third year to complete the project. Scribes and artists, of course, do not spring from the soil; they need to be trained and mentored in the craft—and all to produce copies of the Bible at a sluggish pace.[4]

Materials, expertise, and time—these all made a medieval Bible expensive. Due to the high cost, Bibles produced in the Middle Ages were never sold commercially. If we look for a modern counterpart to medieval Bible production, it would be more like funding a church building campaign. In fact, there are notable cases where monasteries or cathedral churches ran these types of funding campaigns to obtain a complete (and often ornate) copy of the Bible.

The cost of making medieval copies of the Bible raises an important point: Who had access to the Bible? The truth is, the problem of illiteracy among lay Christians was an impossible hurdle for most of Christian history, and the problem increased in the Middle Ages. There were no primary schools as we have today, teaching children to read. So even if the cost of producing a Bible were somehow reduced, the demand for personal Bibles was nonexistent. The lack of access to the Bible was not a result of the church *taking* the Bible from laity, as it was impossible to produce Bibles for every home.

But while this was true, we often hear stories of the Bible chained in libraries, out of reach of laypeople. This is bleak symbolism—fastening a Bible to a shelf under lock and key—and some medieval Bibles were, indeed, locked. Yet while it may sound alarming to modern ears, locked Bibles were not meant to keep away laypeople, but rather to protect the valuable investment of a Bible from thieves. Why would one chain up something of low value?

Gutenberg: Printing Innovation in the Middle Ages

The cost to produce a Bible was out of the church's hands, so any fix would require innovation. The importance of innovation is perhaps the most overlooked feature of many accounts of medieval Bibles. These things may appear remote or archaic by modern standards—sheepskin and quills. We may be more inclined to think of Monty Python and the jokes about the Middle Ages ("How do you know she's a witch?"); countless movies and fairy tales shape our impression of these years too.

There are certainly ways the Middle Ages seem distant from us. This is just as true of the nineteenth century as of the eleventh century. But some of the innovations in Bible production during the Middle Ages were eclipsed only by the invention of computers in the twentieth century. Just as silicon and transistors combined to give us greater access to information, innovations in metal and ink created a market for readers in late medieval Europe that was staggering in comparison with earlier centuries.

Two medieval inventions that improved the cost of Bible production were (1) decreased cost and increased quality of parchment or paper and (2) a way to mass produce the text quickly and uniformly. We will not dwell long on the production of paper or parchment, but suffice it to say, the cost of materials steadily decreased after about AD 1000. The process was slow and likely went unnoticed in those centuries, but historians have noted the trend. Some of these savings were transferred to the merchants who sold Bibles, but they also tended to reduce the cost of Bibles directly.

By far, the most important innovation involved physical printing itself. By the end of the Middle Ages there existed the technical ability to make printed editions of texts. Such technology of a sort existed even in the first century—known as screw presses, which get their name from the machine that screwed a form down onto the medium, allowing for quick and repeatable copies. The trouble with these systems was lack of speed.

To make a page, a printer had to create unique forms for every page, typically carved into wood but occasionally fashioned out of metal. The finished master copy was known as a *platen*—which corresponds roughly to the glass top used in modern photocopiers. To use modern printing language, the process involved making a permanent typeset page, each by hand, so the printer could press each page. Obviously, to make enough platens for a book would require labor and craftsman skill, long hours, and careful planning. One did not make a printed page with haste. One also needed materials beyond merely pen and vellum to make a Bible— and since books were produced for profit, there needed to be a known market of buyers for the finished texts. This explains why the copying of texts by hand endured for so long.

What happened in the 1400s, though, would rapidly take Europe by storm. The man credited with the invention is Johannes Gutenberg (c. 1400–1468), a blacksmith and business-savvy man from the city of Mainz in Germany. We are not sure what led to the invention, but some have speculated that Gutenberg noticed the pressing of cloth by similar form presses. The invention, though, was not the press itself but rather a unique and ingenious way to quickly create different *platen* for a collected book. The invention is known as movable-type printing.

We must recognize, though, that this language is historically slippery. We are accustomed to saying that Gutenberg invented the movable-type press—and often it is implied that this was something never seen in human history. As we just noted, Gutenberg was not without examples of screw presses and presses in other industries. Movable type was also featured in Chinese and Korean printing centuries earlier, though Gutenberg would not have known this. Gutenberg often gets all the credit for something that instead lay dormant before he leveraged technology to advance production. The story of Gutenberg, then, is not of a genius who invented something, but of an industrious man who shaped the way printing could be used to quicken book production, increase sales, and create a new industry of bookmaking.

Gutenberg developed what we might describe as a page outline, or grid, that was used to make a variety of typeset pages. Letters or words could be fashioned out of wood or metal; these pieces could then be arranged within the grid to create each page, only now the pages were temporary. Rather than carving or smithing entire pages, the printer could make the pages with ease. There was also no longer a need for craftsman-level skill, as even an apprentice could arrange the letters. More importantly, errors no longer wasted hours of work; an error now took only a few minutes to correct. After a page was printed, the letters would be removed and letters for the next page (or set of pages) would be arranged in the same form.

The use of movable type, or individual metal letters, is the real miracle of the Gutenberg printing press. Production time dropped to a mere fraction of what it took to produce books before. Costs quickly dropped too. What had formerly cost roughly the price of a house was now estimated at a week's wages.

The choice of text for Gutenberg was relatively easy: the Bible was always in high demand. Churches, monasteries, and nobility also had the means to pay publishers and copyists. The possibility of offering a cheaper supply for the same demand was ideal, with the likelihood of expanding into newer markets with the emerging middle class.

The Bible before Luther

As we have seen in this chapter, the Bible was cherished in the medieval world—not only because it was God's Word, but because of the staggering cost associated with producing a complete copy. Each of these Bibles would, of course, appear strange to us. Their language is not our own, but even the materials used to make these Bibles are unlike any book we have ever purchased. But we must not see the thousand years between the time of the early church and the time of the Reformation as a Bibleless era. Though in different shapes, pages often made from the skin of animals, with words carefully printed by monks, their Bibles were the same as ours.

Study Questions

1. Have you ever tried to copy an entire book of the Bible (or a chapter even)? If so, did you find it difficult to do by hand?
2. We can own personal Bibles and read them whenever we choose. Medieval lay Christians could not. How do you think this affected their faith?
3. Medieval Bibles often look like pieces of art. Should Bibles have art like this to make them beautiful, or should they only include the biblical text? Explain.

Recommended Reading

De Hamel, Christopher. *The Book: A History of the Bible*. London: Phaidon, 2001.

Van Liere, Frans. *An Introduction to the Medieval Bible*. Cambridge: Cambridge University Press, 2014.

CHAPTER 8

THE RENEGADE BIBLE OF JOHN WYCLIFFE

We turn now to one of the most important parts of the Bible's story, particularly for the Bible in English, the creation of the Wycliffe Bible. This Bible comes to us from the Lollard movement — a loose collection of men and women who found inspiration in the protest of John Wycliffe. Like William Tyndale (whom we will discuss in chapter 10), the name *Wycliffe* is today synonymous with the desire to see the Bible translated into spoken languages. This is because he was among the first to stress a biblical faith without a pope—and to stress a Bible in English, not in Latin. In other words, Wycliffe took the notion of a Bible in everyday language and made it a quintessentially anti-Catholic position.

We will look at Wycliffe's approach to the Bible, which was condemned by the Catholic Church. If Wycliffe is a forerunner to the Protestant Reformation, we should understand his view of biblical authority.

Wycliffe was not a man who wished only to see religious change in England. As we shall see, the Lollard movement rode alongside social change in England, where both peasants and the rising middle class began to call for social change. Wycliffe's ideas, in fact, were claimed as the rationale for at least one attempt to overthrow English society—the Peasants Revolt of 1381. The notion of creating an *English* version of the Bible, out of the hands of Catholic leaders, was not simply a call for personal devotion; it was a call for a new England governed by the people. Wycliffe taught that if the Bible was made available to the masses, then the tyrants of their day—both in the church and in society—would find their days numbered.

Above all, Wycliffe inspired a new English translation of the Bible. It was not the best translation and rarely the best production quality. But it was a Bible in English, set over and against the Catholic Church. As such, it created a legacy for early English translations that didn't fully flourish until the sixteenth century, culminating in the King James Bible.

The Problem of the Late Middle Ages

Historians have for the last two generations debated just how bad things got in the last centuries of medieval Europe (AD 1300–1500). Was the church run by a den of thieves, or had only a few wolves slipped in among the sheep? Some historians choose to see a rosier picture of late-medieval Europe, but all scholars admit that things in the Catholic Church were not well. If we are to understand the protest of Wycliffe—and the Bible he inspired—it will be helpful to start by looking at these problems.

The most important issue in the background of Wycliffe's church was the authority of the pope. But the issues in the 1300s went further back to roughly the year 1000. During these centuries, the Catholic Church began to develop new ideas about the pope's authority. The expansion of papal authority was first designed to thwart a series of kings who would not listen to the church. By Wycliffe's day, however, these new ideas on papal authority came to the point that it was now claimed that the Roman Church could not err, that the Bible was not over the pope but rather the pope had the right to *interpret* the Bible for the church.

Where did these ideas come from? In the ancient church, the bishop of Rome, better known as the pope, had always assumed certain privileges, if only for the sake of the importance of the city of Rome. Most of these privileges were never about the authority of the Roman bishop—at least not as the only bishop who could determine doctrine. But by the fourth century, the pope had come to see his role as an *overseer* of churches beyond his diocese.

Yet as time wore on, those who held the papal office became weak (often controlled by a handful of Italian families) and sometimes corrupt. If this was the vicar of Christ, the papacy in the early medieval period was hardly worthy of this title. At one point in the tenth century, in fact, the situation was bad enough to be dubbed the *Pornocracy*. Lurid stories of murder, sex, and treachery were everywhere.

By the year 1000, a series of popes began to push against kings and princes who attempted to control the Roman Curia, the administrative organization of the Holy See. Pope Gregory VII (c. 1072–85) embodied this new aggressive style of leadership as pope. In 1075 he issued the *Dictatus Papae*, a series of blistering decrees that threatened to dethrone any political ruler who interfered with Catholic business, as well as excommunication for the clergy who supported these rulers. The articles stated that only the pope may make laws for the church, and even said that the church of Rome had never erred (and never could err) on matters of faith. Political rulers were instructed to kiss the feet of the pope when coming into his presence. The pope was now over both church and politics.

This development in papal authority culminated in 1302, when Boniface VIII—one of the most notorious popes of the late medieval period—issued *Unam Sanctam*. Boniface stressed many of the same points as Gregory, especially the claim that the pope was sovereign over the kings of Europe. He took the additional step, however, of giving the theological rationale for this teaching, saying that since spiritual matters were superior to worldly matters, the pope's authority was superior to all worldly authority.

Not a few kings crossed swords with the pope during these centuries—not always to their benefit. King Henry IV, emperor of the Holy Roman Empire, did so against Gregory and wound up outside the pope's residence, pleading to have the sentence of excommunication lifted. Like Henry, other rebellious kings soon fell in line behind the Catholic Church. These issues are not irrelevant when it comes to the protest of Wycliffe.

Another problem for the Catholic Church was the papal schism—history books sometimes call it the Western Schism—that erupted in 1378. As the name implies, this was a split between rival popes, each claiming the authority of Rome. It was catastrophic, and it occurred when Wycliffe was beginning to champion reform in England.

The main issue that led to the schism was the Avignon Papacy. The name comes from the city of Avignon in southern France, and it refers to a period of seventy-six years when the French king seized control of the papacy, moving its courts to the city of Avignon. In a sense, the papacy became part of the French government. When the pope wrestled free of the king's grasp and returned to Rome in 1378, that same year a schism erupted among the cardinals during selection of the next pope. The French cardinals—powerful voices after being so long in France—were threatened physically by local citizens in Rome, who wanted to see an Italian chosen for the next pope. Not willing to suffer bodily for French dominance, the cardinals were prudent and elected Bartolomeo Prignano to be Urban VI. The French cardinals were unhappy with the outcome and fled to Anagni in central Italy, declared the decision void, and elected a new pope—Clement VII.

What the French cardinals had not considered was that they lacked the muscle required to remove Urban VI, who was duly elected, even if under pressure. He refused to step down and, as a result, the Catholic Church was run for the next twenty-six years by two popes, each elected from the cardinals. At one point, after a failed attempt to elect someone else, three different popes claimed the authority of Rome.

Thus, the papacy's growing claims of authority alongside the splintering of the office made the protest by Wycliffe particularly relevant. To put it bluntly, anyone who wished to criticize the papacy had ample reason to do so.

Wycliffe the Statesman

John Wycliffe was not a man of the people. He was an intellectual and was involved in politics, as he had become close friends with John of Gaunt, the son of King Edward III (1312–77). He would have been as comfortable hearing a conversation in Latin as in Anglo-Norman, a dialect spoken at the time by the nobility that blended French and older English. The English spoken at that time was Middle English—what would have sounded to our ears like a mixture of gibberish and a thickly accented English dialect. For example, the preface to the Wycliffe Bible says that the translators wanted the Bible in the *"modir tunge of her owne."* This was the English used by Chaucer in *Canterbury Tales*. It descended from the Germanic language of the Anglo-Saxons.

The contrast between English and Anglo-Norman points to a stark division between the English rulers and the people. After the Norman Conquest in 1066, England had been heavily influenced by medieval French language and culture—which we can see today in the number of words that have needless French synonyms: chicken/poultry, pig/pork, lord/liege, smell/odor, buy/purchase. These words borrowed from the French suggest a deeper influence, at least among the nobility. The peasants of England, however, were the labor force that kept the economy going. They almost always spoke English, but they also grumbled at how their work was exploited by local rulers. A way to remember this is that the story of Robin Hood—stealing from the rich to give to the poor—emerged in England around this time.

Wycliffe was born in the far north of England, in the region known as North Riding Yorkshire. His family was at least comfortable, if not wealthy. They had enough wealth through clergy benefits to send Wycliffe to study at Oxford, the city where he would base the early years of his career. His days at Oxford were alive with several important events. The first is the popularity of Thomas Bradwardine, the Archbishop of Canterbury, who had published *On the Cause of God against the Pelagians* a few decades earlier. Bradwardine can be seen as a medieval Calvinist—or at least a fervent Augustinian—who stressed the immediate providence of God over all things. His book was likely a deep influence on the thinking of Wycliffe.

Another event at Oxford was the notorious St Scholastica Day riot (1355)—one of the earliest examples of town-and-gown problems. The tensions that caused the riot, though, were similar to those at work in all of England: the friction between men of wealth and the working classes. In this case, two students complained to a tavern owner about the quality of his beer. The owner responded with some choice words, at which point the students threw the beer in his face. A fight erupted, spilled into the street, and led to several days of looting, property destruction, and armed standoffs between city and university people. A total of two-thousand people, including sixty-five scholars, were killed. Clearly, the fight was not just about the beer.

Not that these events directly provoked Wycliffe to launch his reform movement. But they do speak to the deeper tensions in England—issues of wealth and power—that were made worse by the arrival in Europe of the Black Death. The plague is infamous even today, as it wiped out nearly a third of the population of Europe—with estimations between 75 million and 200 million deaths from 1346 to 1353. The city of Florence, for example, experienced staggering losses, the population dropping from 120,000 residents to between 30,000 and 40,000. Overwhelming numbers of deaths caused further loss of confidence among the survivors: it is impossible to dig mass graves and still believe that all is right in the world.

What we know of Wycliffe's early thinking suggests he was enormously preoccupied with the return of Christ. His teachings on this are unique for medieval theology. In his first book, *The Last Age of the Church* (1356), he seems to teach that the world was nearing the return of Christ. We are not sure how long he continued down this path, and he may have abandoned the matter.

But this is at least a sign that, in his youthful days, Wycliffe was unhappy enough to think that the world was on the verge of an apocalypse.

Wycliffe's general approach to theology reaveals his discontent with the Catholic Church. He stressed that Christians have immediate access to God through Christ, not a faith that can gain access to God only through the church. Such an idea is almost impossible to find in medieval theology, and it tells us how different Wycliffe was. Indeed, if there is any single idea in Wycliffe's theology, it is that *all institutions* are inherently flawed. For example, in his early years, he weighed in on several political discussions, and he consistently stressed the problem of vice and corruption—the tendency of those with unchecked power to become abusive.

When his mind turned to theological matters, he stressed the same points. As a teacher at Oxford, he began to draw large numbers of students who appreciated his teaching against the church's abuse of power. At the same time, Wycliffe increasingly began to see the Bible as the only source of comfort for the faithful, and he grew more caustic with those who spoke of papal authority. As we noted earlier, this was a time when the papacy inspired few Christians. In 1381, when an envoy from one of the schismatic popes arrived in England, Wycliffe delivered an address to Parliament against England's siding with any of the existing popes. Christians, he argued, do not need the blessing of a human for salvation.

We again must emphasize how different Wycliffe's teaching was in the context of the medieval church. Others called for reform, but their calls focused on internal reform, seeking to recover an earlier holiness perceived to be part of the earlier medieval church. Wycliffe, by contrast, wished to undercut the entire foundation of the Catholic Church. His complaints about the church were not trivial. In fact, they were touchstone issues that would be raised again in the Reformation—the most important being the authority of the papal magisterium to determine the official doctrine of the church. Wycliffe came to see papal authority not as a support to biblical faith, but as a threat to true Christianity. His solution to this problem was to return to a Bible-only faith, and for that England would need a Bible in her mother tongue.

The Wycliffe Bible

Wycliffe was not the first to believe the Bible should be available in a language understandable to the people. Even the Vulgate, ironically, was created to be a vernacular translation. But the medieval church lacked the desire or the infrastructure to translate into new languages. These new languages had, by 1300, clearly emerged in Europe, and they began to look increasingly like their modern counterparts: German, French, Dutch, English, and so forth.

The importance of Wycliffe's Bible was not that he launched the first campaign to have the Bible in a language spoken by the people. Wycliffe's Bible was not even the first translation of the Bible into English. Several copies of the Gospels, even handwritten translations of the entire Bible, are known to have existed, though they were not widely available. In a sense, the Catholic Church operated with a contradictory set of principles: it affirmed the Bible was for all Christians, yet it valued the Vulgate as the translation for worship. Most of Europe was still illiterate at this time, so the main place they heard the Bible was in church. Those who led the services were educated, so the Latin of the Vulgate was not an obstacle for them as it was for the people.

What set apart the translation supervised by John Wycliffe was the animosity between Wycliffe and the Catholic Church. That animosity inspired others in England—only a few, but enough to provoke rumors of greater numbers—to join Wycliffe in opposing the role of the pope in medieval doctrine and practice. Wycliffe's sympathizers became known as the Lollards—a name that may have come from a Dutch word that means "*nonsense.*" The joke was that the Lollards mumbled their words, which they had learned in their handmade Bibles.

These Lollards are hard to pin down, as there is only fragmented evidence of their whereabouts. It is likely that they were never more than a loose jangle of individuals who kept their Bibles out of sight of Catholic authorities. But what they shared with Wycliffe was the principle that the Latin Bible—Jerome's Vulgate—was part of the problem with the Catholic Church. The complaint was not that the Vulgate was full of errors, but that only the clergy could understand its language. Lacking an understanding of the Bible, the church was drifting from its foundations. And like Wycliffe, the Lollards began to cry for having the Bible in English. None of them uttered anything like the Reformation slogan of *sola scriptura*—"the Bible alone"—but they came near enough to this belief. The Bible, they believed, should be available to all Christians, read in a language they could understand, to keep the church's teachers in check.

The Wycliffe Bible itself emerged over a period of time, and it was not the work of Wycliffe exclusively. Wycliffe was the overseer of a project that slowly translated the Bible from the Vulgate into English between 1382 and 1395. The two earliest copies we have are housed in Oxford. They are tight on the page, heavily abbreviated, and hard to read by today's standards. For a medieval manuscript, it was a typical example of such books, though it was not at this point a book that would be used by the people. More likely it was used by pastors or preachers who could read, and now could read the Bible in English instead of Latin. In places, the translation was a word-for-word rendering of the Latin—not always done well. For example, the Vulgate reading of Genesis 1 says *et facta est lux* ("and there was light"). The grammar here in Latin combines the two verbs and should be rendered simply *"and the light was made."* But, as many students of a new language can understand, the translators of the first Wycliffe Bible chose to simply render each word into English in the same order: *maad is ligt* ("made is light"). Overall, the Wycliffe Bible was not a bad translation, but it was clearly the work of those new to the task.

The Wycliffe Bible went through several revisions, the most notable the work of John Purvey and Nicholas Hereford, though we cannot rule out that others freely adapted the original Wycliffe Bible. The many copies we have of the Wycliffe Bible today come from this later period. Some are ornate, clearly intended for the wealthy to use. Some of the English nobility may have owned a copy. Possession of the Bible was allowed in restricted cases so long as it wasn't used to undermine Catholic authority. The issue for Wycliffe was always how the Bible was to be used—as a catalyst for social change, for a new vision for the church, or for personal devotion within the bosom of Mother Church.

Social Upheaval

A final word can be said about how Wycliffe's ideals were expressed in the fourteenth century. As we saw earlier in this chapter, Europe as a whole, and England in particular, experienced friction between the social classes. These classes had arisen slowly in the West, largely as feudalism came into existence, and with it the social hierarchy of lords over peasants. When the Lollard movement began, there were some who could not help but see a chance to overhaul English society. (A similar conclusion would be reached by early Lutheran followers.) If Wycliffe was saying the problem with power is that it grows into an oppressive regime, then perhaps all regimes should be removed.

In 1381, the Peasants Revolt—also called Wat Tyler's Rebellion—exploded across England. High taxation and extortion methods to collect these taxes were only a few of the problems. What is interesting for our story is that those inciting violence in England based their actions on the teachings of Wycliffe. Perhaps this was a ploy to gain protection from someone in power—Wycliffe had not yet been condemned—but the circumstances seem to suggest they were telling the truth. Wycliffe himself was uninvolved, but his name was now associated with the violence. The uprising raged on until soldiers were summoned, killing a total of fifteen-hundred rebels.

The Wycliffe Bible was a jumping-off point for how the Bible would be used in the West. Though the Lollard movement itself did little to change England—only a handful of Lollards were left by the start of the English Reformation two centuries later—their role in using the Bible as a tool for social change is one we still see today. We are quite comfortable with the juxtaposition of so many uses for the Bible—held aloft by speakers at political assemblies and at protest marches *against* the government. At times the Bible has been used as a tool for social conformity in the West and was preached by Martin Luther King Jr. at a rally to end segregation. The point is not to imply that the Bible is a wax nose, its message bent to every social view, but to note that Christians since Wycliffe believe the Bible *ought* to be used to bring about change—and that change can come by opposing the powerful institutions in our world. The Bible returned to the center of Christian life, and those who sought to impose laws on the church—and society—could be held accountable to the Word.

Study Questions

1. Why did Wycliffe feel so at odds with powerful institutions?
2. Do you think Wycliffe was right that the Bible should be used to challenge authority? Why or why not?
3. Identify several issues in the church that Wycliffe cited as problems.
4. What do you think is the legacy of Wycliffe in our own day?

Recommended Reading

Brake, Donald L. *A Visual History of the English Bible*. Grand Rapids: Baker Academic, 2008.

Bruce, F. F. *The English Bible*. Oxford: Oxford University Press, 1961.

Lahey, Stephen E. *John Wyclif*. Great Medieval Thinkers. New York: Oxford University Press, 2008.

CHAPTER 9

THE BIBLE AND THE REFORMATION

One of the more prominent differences between Protestants and Catholics is their understanding of biblical authority. Almost universally, at least in its early centuries, the Protestant church has taught that the Bible alone is the authority in matters of the faith—a principle often referred to as *sola scriptura*.[1] Not that Scripture ever stands alone without other, lesser authorities, but that only Scripture can determine Christian practice and doctrine. Catholics teach that the Bible is authoritative, though they believe the papal magisterium also has the authority to rule on doctrine and tradition. These are not small differences.

Our goal here is not to wade into these deeper waters. But it is important to understand certain differences between Protestant and Catholic Bibles. For example, in the modern world, Protestants have chosen almost unanimously to reject the Apocrypha. From the beginning, Protestant Bibles also typically included marginal notes, prefaces, and summaries—features still found in modern versions. Protestants also strove to base their translations on the Greek and Hebrew, not the Latin Vulgate. They typically scorned the Vulgate, not for its own sake but for how it was championed by Catholics. By contrast, Catholics not only continued to use the

Vulgate, but protected it at the Council of Trent as the only text allowable for the study of Scripture. Catholics also rarely included marginal or textual notes in their Bibles, as the need to define their confessional identity was not a serious pressure within their communities. Doctrine was promulgated from Rome.

The issues that divided Protestants from Catholics—the struggle that shaped the Reformation—are therefore part of the story of our Bible. This chapter will explore these issues and look at the rising tide of biblical scholarship in the sixteenth century, resulting from both the recovery of ancient manuscripts and the humanist desire to focus on biblical languages.

Humanism and the Bible

The most influential movement at the end of the Middle Ages was humanism. The movement coincided with the new *study of the humanities* (*studia humanitas*), which drove a wedge between early modern Europe and the ancient Greco-Roman world. The result was that many came to see the medieval period, nearly a thousand years of church history, as a time of intellectual erosion. Indeed, it was a humanist—Francesco Petrarch (1304–74)—who coined the phrase the *Dark Ages*, that horrid time of blood eagles, low literacy, and the Black Death.

What we know as *humanism* arose in the fourteenth century, though it was not a single movement but a cluster of individuals who wished to revive the glory of the classical age of the Greeks and Romans.[2] Above all, humanism was an approach to learning. It was not a worldview or confession—like Platonism or Wesleyanism—but rather a life centered on the love of antiquities. Overall, humanists found the achievements of the Middle Ages to be simplistic or thickheaded. The classical age had been a time of both learning and beauty, but to humanists the medieval world was rather grim. For this reason, humanists loved to lampoon not only medieval scholasticism but those in their day who still adhered to its form of education.

If we think of humanism as an educational model, then we can more easily understand what united all the various forms of humanism (art, poetry, literature, languages, and history). Humanists attempted to breathe new life into each of these fields by going back to the classical age, studying their styles and methods, and then reintroducing these elements to their own generation. For a painter and sculptor like Michelangelo, this meant rediscovering and expanding the field of art and craftsmanship. However, for those interested in the study of the Bible, it meant going back to the original texts, to the languages of Greek and Hebrew. And with this journey back to the sources—*ad fontes*[3] as it was known—came the study of language and the rise of a new approach to the study of Bible manuscripts.

Yet the desire to return to the original sources of the Bible carried with it a dangerous idea. If there was an advantage in knowing the language of the Bible, there was an implied disadvantage in using the Vulgate. The Bible used throughout the Middle Ages—the translation that had become the exclusive version of the Bible for the West—was deemed by many humanists to be inadequate for true biblical studies. They did not agree on what the faults of the Vulgate actually were, and often their jokes about Jerome's bad Latin disguised a weak rationale for why it failed. For some humanists, the Vulgate was fine and a stepping-stone but still only a translation. For some, however, the flaws in Jerome's translation—whether from Jerome missing a grammatical point of

Greek or Hebrew or simply from the difficulty of translating the Bible into any language—created a new level of anxiety. Others did not fault his meaning but found Jerome's style to be misshapen and lackluster. Humanists were irked when Cicero or Virgil read better than their Bibles. And so the study of Greek and Hebrew became to humanists a required field of study.

Not everyone in Europe agreed. The authorities of several of the most influential universities in Europe—Paris, Cologne, and Louvain—resisted the claim that we must know any language other than Latin. Greek was the language of the Eastern Orthodoxy—a branch of the church they considered schismatic and possibly heretical. Hebrew was the language of the Jews—and this was an age still steeped in anti-Semitism. In 1521 a monk in the city of Freiburg (in modern-day Germany) overheard muttering that those who spoke in the Hebrew tongue were, over time, converted to Judaism itself. Not everyone felt this way, but with the study of Hebrew many of the most influential voices in Europe were critical.

Because of this mixture of pride in the Latin Vulgate and a bias against foreign languages, it became the norm to consider the study of Greek and Hebrew a dangerous trend. At the very least, it was considered insolent to claim that centuries of the Christian church had been weak because they failed to parse verbs and nouns well.

The humanist movement fought back with a deluge of publications, some quite serious, others barbed with humorous ironies about rejecting the study of the Bible. Some of the jokes stung the academic community. Universities such as Paris had fought hard to earn their academic freedom, and now the humanists were attempting to shame them for making a power play. In the end, it never made a lot of sense to suggest there was harm in studying the biblical languages. If it aided in the study of the Bible, why all the concern?

But there was a great deal of concern. For example, the first Hebrew grammar published for Christians was known as *The Rudiments of Hebrew* (*De Rudimentis Hebraicis*), published in 1506 by Johannes Reuchlin. By the standard of modern Hebrew scholarship, the book was a labor of love but not a full grammar. (The study of Hebrew would lag somewhat behind Greek, picking up speed only later in the sixteenth century.) The book opened with a dozen or so pages on grammar, but the rest of the book was only a study in word roots and their meaning. It is hard to believe that anyone would master Hebrew with such a book without a tutor. But for a world unaccustomed to the Hebrew language, it opened a new field of study. One could now compare the Hebrew text of the Old Testament, noting especially the meaning of key words, with the text of the Vulgate, since scholars at this time were still fluent in Latin. The only problem was the grammar—and by extension Reuchlin, who was soon accused of heresy.

Reuchlin eventually carried the day, though not without having to appear before the Inquisition in 1513. Still, the humanists of the early 1500s learned through Reuchlin's struggle two important truths. First, if they were to make headway in the study of biblical languages, they would have to set their teeth against the opposition of traditional academics. Second, they were going to have to make it clear that the Vulgate was not only flawed but fixable—but only if Bible scholars used Greek and Hebrew. To achieve both of these goals, the humanists would need a leading voice, someone whose intellectual prowess was without blemish.

Two notable exceptions to the hostility toward biblical languages could be found in Spain and Italy. Both had sizable populations of Jews—although Spain was on the verge in the late 1400s of expelling the Jews during the Reconquista. Large cities in both countries had a combination of humanists and printing shops. Around the turn of the century, a group of publishers, working first in Naples and then in Brescia, in northern Italy, produced complete editions of the Masoretic text of the Hebrew Bible. The edition from Brescia is perhaps the most important, issued in two stages in 1492 and 1494. This edition of the Hebrew Bible was used by both early Protestant churches: by Luther, in the translation of the Old Testament into German, and by Zwingli and Conrad Pellican in Zürich in the early Reformed movement. We still have Luther's personal copy of the Hebrew Bible, in fact, which is kept in Berlin today. Both of these developments—the wellspring of biblical studies and the hard labors to create Protestant Bibles— could not have occurred were it not for the humanist movement.

Erasmus and the Study of Greek

After learning lessons from the Reuchlin affair, the man who took up the struggle for biblical languages was Erasmus of Rotterdam (1466–1536). Famous even in his own day, Erasmus has always been known as the prince of the humanists. He may just as well be called the last of the humanists in terms of humanism's critical edge against traditional Catholicism. Working diligently to overthrow the crusty opinions of Catholic universities, Erasmus appeared to kick open the door for the Reformation. The church had always said, "Attack the Vulgate, let in heresy." And with Luther and other Protestant churches leaving the Catholic faith, it appeared that such predictions were accurate.

In his early years, however, Erasmus was much the same as Reuchlin. He worked tirelessly to recover lost texts, not only of the Bible but also critical editions of the church fathers. His work on the publication of a Greek New Testament was perhaps his most influential contribution, but he also discovered that a series of texts attributed to Augustine were not actually his works. Here was another intellectual pruning away the dead branches of history.

Erasmus was especially concerned with the study of the Bible. Almost from the beginning of his career, he found the Vulgate to be a poor translation. If Erasmus were to cite his main quarrel with Jerome, it would have been that the Latin lacked refinement and polish. Should not the Bible be translated so that it is both faithful to the original language and beautiful in its new language?

Erasmus spent a large amount of time working in the biblical languages, especially Greek. So influential was his role among other humanists that it would be easy to mistake Erasmus as the man who single-handedly rediscovered the study of Greek. This is an overstatement, but he did offer to Europe a model of how one could be deeply pious, faithful to the Catholic Church, yet also a student of biblical languages.

But why the focus on language? As we have noted in previous chapters, Hebrew was rarely studied by Christians after the early centuries of the church. Knowledge of Greek had not been entirely lost in the Middle Ages, but it certainly was not a subject of much study. In the centuries before Erasmus, it may *appear* to us to have been entirely lost. But there were always individuals who—either through education or because of their career—could at least read Greek. Catholic officials who served as ambassadors to the East needed to know Greek or hire someone who did. What had been lost by the time of Erasmus, however, was a knowledge of the bones of Greek: not only the grammar but the style and nuance of the language. To use a modern analogy, it would be one thing to take a German course to be able to read a German newspaper, another to learn to *communicate* in the language. The medieval world had plenty of access to Greek and many knew the language. What it lacked were zealous students of the language who could appreciate its complexity.

Erasmus was not the first to study Greek, nor was he the first to inspire others to do so. Rather, Erasmus gave humanists the *tools* to apply their passion for biblical languages.

In our world, we can take for granted the quality and variety of free online educational materials at our disposal. In Erasmus's day, if you wanted to learn biblical Greek, not only would you have to find a tutor, but you would need access to the Greek New Testament. Greek manuscripts existed in Europe, especially after the fall of Constantinople in 1453, when many Greek-speaking theologians fled to the West. (As good academics, they packed their books before fleeing.) In some cities, these manuscripts would be available for scholars. But while accessing the Greek New Testament was not impossible, the cost and travel associated with such a pursuit lowered the chances that such a field of study would ever become widespread.

Perhaps the first attempt to create a resource for the study of biblical languages is the Complutensian Polyglot—a rather strange name for an important book that never fully made an impact, since it arrived after the Reformation. Why is this text so important? The simplest explanation is that it points in the direction biblical research was going—and where Erasmus eventually landed.

The work was championed by Francisco Ximénes de Cisneros (1436–1517), who was first archbishop of Toledo and then cardinal.

Enormously well connected to Emperor Charles V, Ximénes founded a university in the city Alcalá, near the city of Madrid. The university was to focus on the three languages of Latin, Greek, and Hebrew, but to achieve this lofty goal, Ximénes developed the idea of a single resource, spread across five volumes (the sixth was to be a collection of resources like dictionaries, lists of word roots, and grammar helps). The goal of this massive work was simply to aid biblical students—not unlike educational software or databases that aid students today.

A polyglot is a book of many languages (literally, "many tongues"), and the work was to rival the *Hexapla* made by Origen in the third century. Each page was printed with six columns. The Vulgate was in the middle of the page—like Christ hanging between two thieves, the preface suggested—and on either side are the relevant Greek, Septuagint, or Hebrew texts. Going further than all other study manuals, the Complutensian Polyglot also has each Latin word carefully aligned with its appropriate Greek parallel. The Hebrew text was fixed with a letter that corresponded to the line breaks in the Vulgate. When pertinent to the text, the Aramaic version—then known as Chaldean—was placed in a squat paragraph at the bottom, with a literal translation into Latin beside it.

To anyone not inspired by ancient languages, such a resource sounds like a nightmare. For those passionate about such study, however, this would have been a work crafted for the glorious purpose of spending long nights in the library as young humanists clawed their way into the original languages. Here was a resource, not only with parallel texts, but with extensive aids for anyone stumped by a passage. The cruel fact, however, is that production was suspended just as the pages were printed and ready for binding, shipping, and sales. Shortly after, Ximénes died, and with him went the only serious advocate for the Complutensian Polyglot. The volumes began to be sold in the 1520s, but by then the heady days of the Renaissance had given way to the hostility of the Reformation, and any resource from Catholic Spain, centered on the text of the Vulgate, would be rejected by Protestants.

Since few in Europe were aware of a book that was not yet sold, much attention has fallen on Erasmus and the publication in 1516 of his Greek New Testament. The work is monumental and needs no defense. There was already a resurgence of Hebrew printing in Italy in the late 1400s. Erasmus was never truly interested in Hebrew, but he approved of these efforts. Add to this the earlier contribution of Lorenzo Valla, whose work on New Testament manuscripts Erasmus had read in the city of Louvain in the early 1500s. Valla was a notoriously blunt scholar, who in his career had managed to upset the church by proving that an important work—the *Donation of Constantine*—was a forgery, and then suggesting that the Apostles' Creed was not written by the apostles. Both claims were reason enough to draw daggers and go after Valla.

Valla especially hated the Latin style of the Vulgate, and so he studied the Greek manuscripts he could find, all in an effort to prove that Jerome had misunderstood the original text. Once he had enough fodder, Valla published his *Annotations on the New Testament Collected from Various Codices* (1505)—not the best title, but clearly a shot at the established view of the Vulgate.

Valla's work was largely ignored, likely because of his reputation as a firebrand. However, when Erasmus discovered this text, he found himself agreeing with Valla, and he hatched a plan to carry the project further. Where Valla breathed fire, Erasmus offered cool logic. Erasmus was wise enough to avoid openly mocking the Vulgate. Taking on Jerome—a celebrated church father and a saint—was folly. What Erasmus planned instead was to give scholars the Greek text, coupled with his *own* improved Latin translation.

Erasmus's first Greek New Testament was a worthy dream that initially crashed to the ground. It is likely that when Erasmus convinced the printer, Johann Froben, to take the project, neither was fully aware of the complexity involved. When Erasmus arrived at Basel in 1514, he assumed he would find a stock of Greek manuscripts to work from. But there were only seven manuscripts, all of them Byzantine texts from the twelfth century or later, not all of them good copies. Erasmus was able to compare versions of the Gospels and the Epistles—though he had only one copy of Revelation, and that was missing the final page, containing the last six verses in Greek. Erasmus had to translate the Latin to Greek himself. Driven by the demands of the publisher (a millstone around the necks of many authors), Erasmus may have been forced to work too quickly to meet the final deadline. The result—the *Novum Instrumentum* was finally published in March 1516. Overall, the first edition was a mess, with not only problems in the manuscripts but errors in the printing.

Erasmus's goal in publishing the Greek New Testament was not just to foster a greater appreciation of biblical languages. Everyone knew the importance of the Greek, but they assumed also that the Latin Vulgate was a worthy translation, faithful to the original meaning. Erasmus wanted to do away with some of Jerome's translation choices, but he also wanted to produce a better *Latin translation*, more in step with classical style. In this sense, Erasmus was faulting the Vulgate for misunderstanding the original in its word-for-word meaning, while also noting that it failed to achieve the right dynamic equivalent in the Latin.

So, for Erasmus, the Greek New Testament was not simply a Greek New Testament; rather, it was similar to what we today call an *"interlinear text"* (with the original language next to a modern translation to aid the reader). Each page was divided into two columns: on the left, the Greek; on the right, a new translation into Latin by Erasmus. Titled the *Novum Instrumentum*, the book was not even called the New Testament until the second edition in 1519. Erasmus was initially focused on creating a better Latin Bible—his academic contemporaries who read Latin could work through difficult Greek passages by consulting his new translation.

The problems in the first edition were legion, especially in the eyes of scholars who rejected the study of biblical languages. Having suffered the sting of humanist jeers, traditional scholars now howled at the result of Erasmus's New Testament. Erasmus quickly recovered, however, and produced a total of five editions—each an improvement on the previous edition—before his death in 1536.

Luther and the German Bible

Erasmus's Greek New Testament was the text of choice for most Protestant editions of the New Testament. Those who contributed to new vernacular translations—such as Luther's translation of the Bible into German—reached for Erasmus when working on the New Testament. It was at the elbow of most Protestant leaders as they worked on their sermons. It was a pivotal book that came on the eve of a pivotal reformation.

Based on Erasmus's work, the first Bible of the Reformation was Luther's edition of the New Testament—a landmark publication.

Sparked by a controversy over indulgences—which seemed to imply that money was required to receive assurance of salvation—Luther launched Germany into an unplanned reformation. Once the controversy erupted, however, Luther was happy to be the voice crying in the wilderness. The controversy reached a tipping point in 1520 at Luther's trial at the Diet of Worms.[4] Refusing to recant or back down, Luther was excommunicated and sentenced to be executed. With the support of his allies, on his trip home he was whisked away instead to the Wartburg, a fortress-style castle in Eisenach (almost dead center on a map of modern Germany).

Two things quickly changed in Luther's life. First, while Luther would always wear the black robes of a professor, he shed the outward style of monastic practice. He no longer fasted to extreme lengths, and he no longer shaved his face and head in the style of the tonsure. Later pictures of Luther show a man who is thick around the middle and sporting a brambly beard. This may seem unimportant to us, but since Luther was now a former monk, these symbols were not unlike men growing long hair and women burning bras in the 1960s: each displays an open hostility to the way things had been. Luther did the same when he married Katie von Bora, a former nun. Luther was the persona of rebellion against Rome.

The second feature of Luther's time in the Wartburg—equally countercultural—was his translation of the German New Testament. This work would eventually grow to include the translation of the entire Bible into German. More importantly, Luther's translation would go on to have a more profound impact on the German language than any other single text. Even today the impact of Luther's text is not insignificant. For example, when Greece was hit by financial crisis in the 2010s, there were reports that the German government was in turmoil over whether to forgive their debt. Chancellor Angela Merkel is the daughter of a Lutheran preacher, and she and others knew that the word for "debt" in German is *schulden*—the very thing Christ is said to forgive in the Gospels, and the word that was shaped by the German Bible. The long reach of Luther's Bible has not shortened.

As with any important work, however, later history has tended to embellish the story of Luther's Bible. Like the Wycliffe Bible into English, Luther's translation was not the first vernacular translation. In fact, there were roughly a dozen or so German versions published fifty to seventy-five years before the Reformation. None of these translations raised eyebrows among church leaders, but they were not the work of a man condemned as a heretic. The story of Luther's translation is not interesting because it was the first German Bible, but because it was the first of its kind as a *Protestant* Bible. Not that the Bible was slanted in its message, but that it stood like a beacon for the Protestant view that the Bible alone is the authority of doctrine. The rebel with his rebel translation. The fact that it has endured until the present in the German Lutheran church adds to its legacy.

What Luther published in September 1522—almost five years exactly after the posting of the *Ninety-Five Theses*—was the New Testament portion of what would become his full Bible. The main work was done by the time he left the Wartburg, just under a year after he arrived. He brought the draft back to Wittenberg, where he and his colleague Melanchthon went over it carefully. When it finally was published in September, the result was extraordinary. The cost of a book was somewhere between a half and a full gulden—not a terribly large sum of money, and proof that Gutenberg's invention was indeed lowering the cost of printing, as fine copies made by hand during this time would have fetched more than one-hundred gulden.

The work was not perfect, and a December edition was quickly published to amend errors in the text. Despite the flaws, the Bible nearly always sold out with each subsequent printing. The Catholic Church tried to have the Bible condemned and burned—the Council of Trent that met a generation later even threatened publishers who sold any Bible but the Vulgate—but they could not stanch the bleeding in these early years. Luther spent just over a decade expanding the work until, in 1534, the first edition of the Luther Bible was published in Wittenberg.

A few things can be said about Luther's translation. By and large, Luther always attempted to render the text not word for word, but nearly so. When he felt it necessary, Luther would always give an idiomatic equivalent in the German. In one infamous case, he even added to the text. The verse is Romans 3:28: *"For we maintain that a person is justified by faith apart from the works of the law."* Luther could not help but insert his own word—*alone (alleyn)*—so that it now read that we are justified by *"faith alone,"* though this is not in the Greek. Such liberties in translation are rare in Luther's Bible, but not a few people ever since have cried out against Luther, since he seemed to be violating the Protestant view about *sola scriptura*.

Luther opened the door, but soon other Protestants followed. In Zürich, the Bible named after the city—the *Zürich Bible*—arrived in 1536. This Bible was the work primarily of Zwingli, the lead reformer in the city, and his colleague Leo Jud, and Conrad Pellican helped work through the Hebrew. The work is notable for its attention to detail in the translation process, and many Reformed theologians spoke glowingly of it, since it was a rare feat of translational precision. Zwingli was trained as a humanist and worked hard to balance a word-for-word approach with a pleasant style in German. Additionally, the *Zürich Bible* was perhaps the first Bible to include a printed map of Israel. Other Reformed translations soon emerged, such as the French translation of Pierre Olivétan. Olivétan was the cousin of the future reformer John Calvin, and his translation was the first Protestant French version, *La Bible Qui est toute la Saincte escripture*—though the first French New Testament was by the humanist Jacques Lefèvre (c. 1455–1536).

One final version to note is the first Spanish translation of the Vulgate by Casiodoro de Reina in 1569 (though it was not published until 1609). Casiodoro joined a monastery in the 1550s, soon embraced Protestantism, and became a pastor to Spanish refugees in England. His role as a pastor to a community without their own Bible prompted the work that produced the 1569 version that was edited and improved slightly when it was later published. The Bible was called the *Biblia de Oso* (*Bible of the Bear*), though the origin of this name is unclear.

We will look at Protestant English translations in our next chapter, but we can summarize the story so far. The Reformation was always a movement based on the Bible alone. It scandalized Catholic opponents that Protestantism broke up into different movements almost from the beginning, but differences among the reformers were never so great that they clouded their shared belief that all doctrine, life, and worship must be based on the Bible. That fundamental stance—*sola scriptura*—is the reason that Protestant traditions worked tirelessly at the translation and publication of the Bible.

The Catholic Vulgate

The origin of Protestant Bibles is not the only story from the Reformation. As we have seen in this chapter, both Protestants and humanists rejected the Vulgate, not always for its flaws but for its Latin language. Among Protestants, the primary frustration was that the Vulgate unnecessarily excluded the common people from hearing the Word, and because they could not hear the Word they were not fed and often found themselves ruled by the tyranny of priests and bishops.

The Catholic response to Reformation criticisms of the Vulgate was the Council of Trent (1545–63). In the first session, the council issued a number of anti-Protestant decrees, the second of which takes up the Vulgate. The council minced no words, stating that the Vulgate is "the authentic text in public readings, debates, sermons, and explanations; and no one is to dare or presume on any pretext to reject it." The council also stated that personal judgments were not to be valid reasons for rejecting the Vulgate, and they scorned the use of "notes and commentaries." The session went on to declare that the Protestant commitment to *sola scriptura* was theologically wrong. All promulgations made by the Catholic Church—even recent changes—were to be considered equally authoritative with the Bible. The Council of Trent clarified that church decrees, ratified by the pope, were *equal* with the Bible in authority. The difference between Protestant and Catholic teaching on Scripture could not have been greater.

Study Questions

1. Why was humanism so crucial for the Reformation?
2. Why was Luther's Bible so important?
3. Why did the Protestant movements work so quickly to translate the Bible?

Recommended Reading

Bainton, Roland. *Erasmus of Christendom*. Reprint. Peabody, MA: Hendrickson, 2016.

Bobrick, Benson. *Wide as the Waters: The Story of the English Bible and the Revolution It Inspired*. New York: Simon & Schuster, 2001.

Brake, Donald L. *A Visual History of the English Bible*. Grand Rapids: Baker Academic, 2008.

Bruce, F. F. *The English Bible*. Oxford: Oxford University Press, 1961.

CHAPTER 10

THE PROTESTANT BIBLE IN ENGLISH

The story of the slow conversion of England into a Protestant country is not always appreciated today. The Reformation is often remembered as an explosion of evangelical faith in many countries in Europe—and in places like Wittenberg and Zürich, it was an explosion. In the span of a generation, most of Europe would experience the rise of new Protestant churches. In countries like Germany and France, Protestantism flourished.

England was different. At the start of the Reformation, the country was ruled by Henry VIII, a king not only committed to Catholicism but aggressively opposed to any sympathy for Luther. Henry even wrote a theological work against Luther, defending the seven sacraments—and for his efforts, the pope awarded him the title *"Defender of the Faith."*[1]

But then Henry and his wife Catherine could not produce a male heir. Henry blamed himself, then his wife, and finally the pope for allowing him to marry Catherine. She had been his sister-in-law before his brother Arthur died, but the pope had granted a dispensation allowing them to marry. Now the pope refused to grant an annulment, and Henry was white with rage.

In 1534, Henry had himself declared head of the church.

In a surprise twist, Henry remained a convinced Catholic on many doctrinal matters, and he blew hot and cold on the idea of reforming the English church. The story of England and the Reformation, then, was to be the story of his childen, who would waver between Protestantism (Edward VI), Catholicism (Mary I), and back to Protestantism (Elizabeth I).

This tension in England—as it moved from Catholic to Protestant over the course of three generations—is the basis of the story of the Bible in English.

William Tyndale: Rebel Translator

William Tyndale was born in 1494 in Gloucestershire, England. He went on to study Greek at Oxford before moving to Cambridge. At Cambridge, he may have worked for a season with Erasmus, who was there doing pre-work on his forthcoming Greek New Testament. Beyond this sketch, we know little about Tyndale's early life—though as we have seen, this was a world alive with the study of biblical languages. Not only were scholars increasingly diligent to learn Greek—and at least the rudiments of Hebrew—but they increasingly wanted to use these tools to get to the roots of the Bible. Tyndale lived and breathed this same air, and he seems to have had a natural affinity for the languages.

At some point, Tyndale embraced the Protestant faith, though we know nothing of the circumstances. We also know little about his plans for the future. Unlike Luther or Zwingli, however, he was not the pastor of a church or leader in a local community. There were no people to rally around his cry for reform, and he also may have been unwilling to take a public stance, given the hostility in England toward Protestantism. For Tyndale, the Reformation was about the need for the Bible to be in the native tongue of his people—a view shared by Wycliffe before him. England still had statutes, in fact, from Wycliffe's day that made it illegal to pursue any Bible translation or publication. It was against this legislation that Tyndale believed he could effect change for Protestantism.

Sometime in 1522, when the Reformation was in full bloom throughout Europe, Tyndale arrived in London. Though the Reformation was despised by church and crown, they had embraced humanism, and Tyndale felt it was possible to secure the rights to translate the Bible based on the principles of the Renaissance. That same year Luther published the first edition of his German New Testament. Tyndale now wanted to accomplish the same for England.

Prior to the Council of Trent, criticism of the Vulgate was not officially deemed heresy by the Catholic Church. But given the prohibition against English translations of the Bible, Tyndale needed official sanction to begin the work. The man he asked, Cuthbert Tunstall (1474–1559), was the London bishop, and at least willing to hear Tyndale's request. But he was unwilling to allow such an obviously Protestant approach to Bible translation. Mercifully, Tunstall did not immediately have Tyndale arrested but tried instead to dissuade him from these plans, warning him of the consequences should he continue down this road. Tyndale fled England and never returned.

We don't know where Tyndale went after his departure from England. Recent scholars have suggested he went to Wittenberg, yet there is no clear evidence he ever traveled to Luther's city. Wittenberg University records have a certain Englishman named *Daltin*—and at least one historian has claimed this is a letter scramble of the name *Tindal*.[2] But it would be surprising to see him enrolled as a student, since Tyndale had already graduated from Oxford and Cambridge.[3] It is also unclear why he would need to scramble the letters in his name. Whatever the case, Tyndale had read Luther, approved of his message of faith, and shared his desire for reform.

The most likely case is that Tyndale fled to Germany and landed in the region of the Netherlands. During the Reformation, these lands were notorious for the diversity of religious refugees who settled there. Tyndale would have had relative freedom if he kept his head down and drew no attention to himself. The rejection by Tunstall had not dissuaded him, and he began to seek allies for his English Bible translation, eventually securing the partnership of a merchant named Humphrey Monmouth. If the two could find a printer, Monmouth promised to smuggle Tyndale's translation back into England.

About this time in Tyndale's life, we lose track of his whereabouts. By 1525, we know that he was close to completing work on the New Testament, and he had finally retained the services of a publisher in the city of Cologne in Germany. Then everything got fouled up. In one of the closest calls of his life, Tyndale narrowly escaped Catholic officials when, on the eve of the printing, the plan to smuggle Bibles into England was discovered. Tyndale's presence was now exposed, his work lost. He fled Cologne, leaving behind many of his belongings, and had to start from scratch.

Tyndale next landed in the city of Worms—the location of Luther's trial and final stand before the emperor. Historians believe Tyndale must have kept some of his materials (or perhaps he remembered much of his early translation), because the second attempt at editing went quickly. Among the things lost in Cologne was a series of notes and prefaces Tyndale had hoped to publish with the New Testament. This time, either because he did not wish to repeat the work or because he was worried about the authorities catching him, Tyndale rushed the Bible to the printer as a plain text. Thus, the Worms edition of the Tyndale Bible was shorn of its Protestant commentary.

This was a momentous occasion, Tyndale having now published the first English New Testament since Wycliffe. The book was smallish, a size that could be used for personal reading. The smugglers stowed their contraband Bibles and set off for England and Scotland—the first Protestant effort in history to smuggle Bibles into a country that had banned the Scriptures.

The official reaction to Tyndale's translation was a mixture of exasperation and hostility. Bishop Tunstall—the man who had warned Tyndale not to work on an English translation—called the work a "pernicious poison," its presence threatening to rot the soul of England. That same year, 1526, a bonfire was held in London outside St. Paul's Church, and those copies of Tyndale's Bible that had been seized were consigned to the flames.

Henry VIII was equally upset, surprised as he was to see Lutheran sympathies in England. Behind closed doors, the king made sure his lead intellectuals knew to strike back with vigor. They beefed up security at the docks, and several publishing campaigns were launched against Tyndale. The man who would define the printed attack on Tyndale was Thomas More, the leading English humanist of the sixteenth century. Modern history has gotten the story of Thomas More almost entirely backward— pitching him as either a stoic martyr for the sake of conscience or a liberal cynic for the sake of personal freedom. He was neither.

Thomas More was a convinced Catholic, and given that Henry VIII at this time was also a loyal son of the church, the two were natural allies. With Henry's blessing, More launched an attack on the work of Tyndale—the theater of war for humanists as always being the printed page—and published his *A Dialogue concerning Heresies* in 1529. In this work, More noted particular places in Tyndale's translation that could be seen as subtly undermining the Catholic Church—translating the words for "church" as "congregation," for instance, and the word for "priest" as "elder." These are thin legs to stand heresy on, but More and English Catholics did not need marginal notes to know that Tyndale's New Testament was an effort to undermine the Catholic faith.

The response by English authorities was more than mere words. We know that efforts were launched not only to check the cargo of merchant ships but also to order officials at Oxford and Cambridge to quash any Lutheran sympathies among students. Rumors suggested that at least a few of the students—probably *only* a few at this point—had dabbled in reading Luther. A crackdown was ordered.

The important point here is that England was rocky soil for any form of Protestantism to take root. At times, these crackdowns were mostly bluster and snorting, without much in the way of actual oppression. There was no wave of terror in England, though we hear little about Protestants living in England during these years. It is also true that royal authorities were not always good at rounding up the Tyndale New Testament, though enough effort was made that the smuggling soon came to a halt. Whether from book burning or the rust of history, we have only three copies of this first edition, which means that several hundred were lost.

Undaunted by these setbacks, Tyndale continued to work toward his goal of completing his translation. The Old Testament was slower going—due either to the relative challenge of Hebrew or to stress on his time—but in 1530 he released the Pentateuch, followed in 1531 with Jonah. This portion of his translation work was some of his best. For example, the opening chapter of Genesis in English will forever bear his words, *"In the beginning God created the heavens and the earth."* Some other books of the Old Testament were in the works at the time of his death in 1536. We know he had finished at least Joshua, Judges, and both books of Samuel and Chronicles, and he may have completed portions of Ruth. None of these later texts survived, however, and were only incorporated in English Bibles later (see below).

Had Tyndale completed his translation of the Bible, his influence on our modern English Bibles would have been immeasurable. But Tyndale had crossed swords with Henry VIII over his divorce from Catherine of Aragon. Other English Protestants, such as Thomas Cranmer and Hugh Latimer, had sided with Henry that the pope never should have granted the marriage, and they at least held their tongues when the king cast off Catherine and married Anne Boleyn. For Tyndale, however, divorce was far worse than a poor decision to marry your dead brother's wife—and he said so in print. Henry never fully relented from his anger over this, and he stressed to foreign rulers that Tyndale was both a heretic and an enemy of the crown. In 1536, Spanish authorities in Antwerp were alerted to his presence and Tyndale was arrested, put through a hasty trial, and then executed. At the time of his death, he had been working on his translation of the Old Testament prophets.

Tyndale's Bible as a Foundation

The story of Tyndale's Bible—especially how his translation was incomplete because of his martyrdom—should not obscure the fact that Tyndale was the most influential person in the history of the English Bible. In fact, if we consider the influence of Tyndale on all English Bibles ever since—including today—it would only be a slight exaggeration to say that Tyndale has had the most influence on the English language since Chaucer. As one historian has suggested, if it were not for Tyndale, there would have been no Shakespeare.[4] And while students often forget their Shakespeare, the expressions and idioms from the Tyndale Bible are still used today.

Tyndale seemed to have a knack for languages, learning not only Greek and some Hebrew, but perhaps other languages like Italian. He had drunk deep in the study of the humanities, with the desire to understand the Bible in the originals. Of course, we have no accurate way today to measure his mastery of languages, but by the standard of the Reformation, he was a serious Bible scholar.

Tyndale was also immensely gifted at turning a phrase in English—creating a translation that was at times poetic while still being faithful to the original Greek or Hebrew. Examples include his rendering of Revelation 3:20: "*Behold, I stand at the door and knock,*" contrasted with an almost lyrical rendering of Acts 17:28: "*In whom we live and move and have our being.*" Although people today often remember the King James Bible for its rich tones, the King James Version and all other English Bibles borrowed nearly all of Tyndale's New Testament and the portions of the Old Testament he had completed, which is nearly half of the entire Bible. Studies have shown that as much as 90 percent of all modern English translations still reflect the wording used by Tyndale.

Tyndale was also the creator of unique words and idioms that entered the English language. For example, Tyndale crafted the words *Passover* and *scapegoat* for the story of the exodus and the work of Christ in the New Testament. He also brought out the word *atonement,* which was an archaic word rarely used in English. The word itself was a mash-up of two words—*At-One-ment*—and meant the bringing together of two separate things to make them *at-one.* Tyndale reached for the word *atonement* when translating the Hebrew word *kippur*—notably in the Israelite ceremony of the Day of Atonement (*Yom Kippur*). Thus, Christians have Tyndale to thank for giving us one of the most important words to frame the topic of the forgiveness of sin.

Other phrases have become common in English, though some today may not realize they come from Scripture. Just a few examples include: *gave up the ghost, filthy lucre, my brother's keeper, the signs of the times, fight the good fight, the twinkling of an eye,* and *judge not lest you be judged.* We do not use English today without at least the possibility of speaking the words of Tyndale's Bible, which should be one of the most celebrated works of the English language.

After Tyndale

The English Reformation did not die with Tyndale. Although he worked mostly alone—due largely to the fact that no hub or city became the center of English Protestantism—there were others who shared Tyndale's commitment to Protestantism. The first to take up Tyndale's mission to produce an English Bible was Miles Coverdale (1488–1569). A fellow student at Cambridge, Coverdale shared the same love of humanism as Tyndale, especially the study of biblical languages. During his education, he even traveled to the Louvain (in modern Belgium) to study with Erasmus, after the Dutch humanist had left Cambridge. Unlike Tyndale, however,

Coverdale sought a career in the church, and he was later received as a monk into the Augustinian order.

By at least 1527, however, Coverdale had embraced the Reformation. The previous year he had served as secretary and witness in the trial of Robert Barnes, who was accused of Lutheran heresies. Barnes had preached a Protestant-themed sermon at St. Edward's King and Martyr Church in Cambridge—a building often considered to be ground zero for the English Reformation. Several men, including Coverdale, vouched for his orthodoxy before church authorities in London, and they managed to secure his acquittal. Authorities still were not convinced, and Barnes remained under a watchful eye. A decade later things were bleak for Protestants, and the same charges were brought up, only this time Barnes was executed in 1540. The Anglican church was hardened by these martyr stories.

Perhaps due to this pressure in England, Coverdale appears to have been swayed to leave England. Some have suggested he assisted Tyndale in his translation efforts, though we have nothing conclusive in the evidence. Still, it is plausible he at least had contact with Tyndale during these years. After Tyndale's execution, Coverdale decided he should return to England and seek the safety of his country rather than risk capture himself.

Fortune smiled on Coverdale when he returned to London. Unlike Tyndale, he had never been accused of heresy, so he was not being sought by English authorities. But there was also sudden optimism among English Protestants about the chances of swaying Henry to the cause of reform—especially as the 1520s progressed. The problems with Henry's marriage made him an enemy of the pope, and English Protestants knew this shared opposition to Rome could bind the king's heart to their Reformation.

Simply put, it is difficult to account for the staggering change in Henry—from staunch supporter of the pope to at least somewhat open to reform. Many historians have sought the elusive answer that would justify this change, but not a few have run their boats aground in their effort.

The central issue Coverdale and others had to reckon with was Henry's desire to remove England from the Catholic Church. The same king who wrote a book against Luther in 1521—who scorned Protestant views on justification by faith—now in 1534 cast the pope's authority out of England entirely. And yet, scholars are mostly convinced that Henry did not alter much of his theology—at least on issues not related to papal authority. Henry's fight was over the authority of the pope to grant him the right to divorce Catherine of Aragon.

The *"Great Matter"* for Henry VIII—as his divorce is often called—played a central role in the history of the English Bible, since it played the key role in launching England in a Protestant direction. To the end of his days, Henry was still *conservative* in his theology—we might even say he was *Catholic without the pope*, though such a thing is impossible. But the king now found solidarity with a few Protestants, given their mutual animosity toward Rome. At the very least, those who demonstrated their loyalty to the Tudor dynasty—men like Thomas Cranmer—would be given a long leash. If you crossed Henry—as Tyndale had—you would remain a target.

Coverdale easily kept a low profile during these years. Thomas Cranmer and other Protestant leaders had by 1536 convinced Henry to agree to the creation of an English Bible. He refused other reforms, but the Bible spoke of obedience to kings, so Henry found it a good thing for his new English church.

The first person tasked with creating the English Bible was, in fact, Coverdale. In 1535, he produced a Bible in English—the first *complete* English Bible in the Reformation. Today the book is known as the Coverdale Bible, though it was once called the Treacle Bible—given its translation of Jeremiah 8:22: *"Is there not triacle [treacle] in Gilead?"*[5] But it would be wrong to see Coverdale as a *translator*. Instead, he was more of an editor, cobbling together Tyndale's Bible with his own translations from the Zürich Bible, Luther's Bible, and the Vulgate for the remaining portions of the Old Testament not done by Tyndale. Coverdale's only change to Tyndale's translation was to leave out the offensive words *congregation* and *elder*. In terms of usage today, the most notable portion of this Bible is the Coverdale Psalter, which was later incorporated into the *Book of Common Prayer* in 1549, making it the source of so many Anglican prayers over the centuries.[6]

Beyond the Psalter, the Coverdale Bible is largely forgotten today—not only because it was a compilation, but also because it was quickly set aside by Henry. Perhaps due to the heady zeal of the moment—at last to see an official Bible in English—Coverdale had failed to secure the written permission needed from Henry to produce the text, since the king had only given his verbal approval. This was illegal, at least technically, and so Henry was not asked to approve something after the fact. In 1537, a second Bible was produced—nearly identical to the Coverdale Bible—known today as the Matthew Bible (or the Thomas Matthew Bible). The strange thing about this translation is that there was no Thomas Matthew; the work was produced by John Rogers, a man who had assisted Tyndale in Europe.

The Matthew Bible is an example of historical irony for two reasons. First, it was the first Bible in English history that was truly *authorized* by the king—as some mistakenly call the King James Version. More on this in our next chapter.

Second, it was Coverdale and Rogers who largely preserved the Tyndale Bible for later history. Were it not for their willingness to risk King Henry's anger—it's a wonder no one noticed and told the king—the Tyndale Bible likely would have suffered a fate similar to the Wycliffe Bible—remembered only as a story of history. But with Coverdale's translation, now as the Matthew Bible stamped with royal authority, the legacy of Tyndale was passed on to all subsequent English Bibles.

The Great Bible

Henry issued a decree that the Matthew Bible, once completed, was to be placed in every church in England on Easter 1539. Trouble lay ahead, however, as the Bible was sent to Paris to be printed. The Inquisition discovered it and, now that England was a heretical country, stopped production. Work had to start again.

All of this complex story ended later in 1539 when, finally, there was produced the Great Bible, authorized by the king, based on the text of Tyndale, and carried to completion by two of Tyndale's Protestant allies. Thus, the Great Bible was a symbolic link between the earlier work of English Protestants and the King James Bible. Without Henry's final approval, it would not have been an inspiration and source for subsequent Bible translators under both Elizabeth I and James I.

Study Questions

1. What do you find are the major differences between the English Reformation and other Protestant movements?
2. What do you think is the legacy of Tyndale's Bible?

Recommended Reading

Bobrick, Benson. *Wide as the Waters: The Story of the English Bible and the Revolution It Inspired*. New York: Simon & Schuster, 2001.

Teems, David. *Tyndale: The Man Who Gave God an English Voice*. Nashville: Thomas Nelson, 2012.

Tyndale, William. *The New Testament: A Facsimile of the 1526 Edition*. Peabody, MA: Hendrickson, 2008.

CHAPTER 11

THE KING JAMES BIBLE

Go to any Christian bookstore and you will find many different Bible translations, including an almost exhaustive list of every kind of study Bible possible. But even with such choices, nothing can overtake the King James Version in terms of usage by Christians. There may be dozens of English Bibles—far more than any other language—but the KJV still captures the attention of North American readers. Conservative estimates are that as many as 50 to 53 percent of those who read the Bible on a weekly basis reach for a copy of the King James Bible.[1] There is a familiarity with its sound and rhythm—even in a world that has left such language behind.

For this reason, the KJV needs no introduction. It is a Bible with two names—the *KJV* to North Americans, the *Authorized Version* in Britain—neither of which were used when it was printed. The original title page had simply *The Holy Bible*, along with the typical run-on sentence that explained the book's contents. Within a generation of its first edition, however, a virtual monopoly was established with printers, securing its price and transmission over the years and allowing it to become the most read Bible in English for almost three hundred years.

Readers today may find its language clunky or old-fashioned—or at the very least a quaint throwback to the age of Shakespeare. But this estimation cannot erase the fact that the KJV is one of the most influential translations in the history of the English language. In this chapter, we will tell the story of its origin while also dispelling a few of its myths.

The Battle for Anglicanism

The history books tell us that the reign of James I was a dark and brooding time. Religious oppression and conformity were the patterns established by the king, and those who crossed him would lose their churches. The fabled story of the first Thanksgiving—with pilgrims sharing popcorn with Native Americans—shares parallels with the great myths of King James's reign. We often can't help but think of them as huddled masses, yearning to breathe free, hoping to escape the dank dungeons of England. Depending on the source, these stories make it sound as if Jacobean England was a kind of Stalinist Russia.

Such vivid imagery is not likely to fade, but it is the product of imagination, not historical fact. Tensions certainly existed between the king and the church—or more specifically between the king and *certain* reformers within the church. But these tensions had been part of English history since the 1550s. The most important question—indeed the only question that mattered at the time—was how much reform was needed in the English church.

Everyone knew England was, by the time of Elizabeth, a Protestant nation. In terms of worship, England had no pope and two sacraments. The *Thirty-Nine Articles*—the confession of the English church—affirmed not only justification by faith but predestination and marriage of priests, and they stressed that the Bible should be published without the Apocrypha.[2] They also condemned Catholic teachings on purgatory, good works, and praying to saints. The *Articles* went further, noting that the Church of Rome had erred on the most crucial matters of biblical faith. The point was obvious: Anglicanism was no halfway house for Catholics.

It was, however, a middle road between the other Reformation movements—the Lutheran and Reformed churches. Anglicanism retained elements in its reformation that others, especially the Reformed churches, had thrown out. The leaders of the English Protestant church did not view this as a betrayal of their Protestant faith, and they often reminded their Reformed friends of their shared doctrinal positions on almost every issue.

The sticking point, though, was Anglican worship. Those who rejected the Anglican form of worship were often from the Reformed camp (sometimes called Calvinists[3]). The driving force for most Reformed churches was a zeal for purity, especially in the case of worship. Ironically, both sides shared a common theological perspective; they just had different applications of their theology in regard to worship. In one famous case—the debates in the 1560s over priests wearing vestments—both sides cited the same sources against one another. This friction was, in a sense, a quarrel among siblings.

Why did it come to this? A good way to understand this struggle is to see the pain involved for Reformed pastors. The Catholic faith was not simply a different denomination. In the sixteenth century, many of the early leaders of Anglicanism had suffered martyrdom or exile—losing either life or property for the sake of the Reformation. When the exiles returned, it stung them to see Anglican priests wearing robes that appeared Catholic. Much like political exiles today who have fled oppressive nations, the Reformed Puritans found it loathsome to identify any longer with old patterns of life. Reformed pastors no longer wanted to even *appear* Catholic—even when they agreed that robes were themselves a nonessential issue. Friends had been burned at the stake and loved ones had lost their homes for the sake of leaving the Catholic faith. Why would they want to continue these practices? Even those who disagree with this point can understand the stress.

The leaders of the English church, especially Elizabeth I, did not agree with such a harsh stance on changing worship. In their minds, the beauty of traditional practices, if they were not contrary to the Bible, could be retained without superstition. For example, take the practice of kneeling in worship. On its own, kneeling is certainly a biblical practice—Jesus himself knelt in the garden of Gethsemane. However, medieval Catholics had knelt in devotion to all sorts of religious services that Protestants now rejected, such as the adoration of the bread and wine during Mass. Reformed pastors felt there was always a twinge of superstition for those who continued to kneel in worship—and they would rather not flirt with the old corruptions that had ruined the Catholic Church.

These tensions drove Puritans and Anglicans, as we call them today, to squabble over things like robes, wedding rings, bowing before the cross, and making the sign of the cross. *Everyone* admitted these things, on their own, were inconsequential for worship (they used the term *adiaphora*, or things indifferent). But early Puritans insisted these issues were dangerous for the church. Priestly robes were nothing but cloth, except when they reminded the worshiper of the dregs of papal superstition.

Two Bibles came to define the struggle between Anglicans and Puritans: the Geneva Bible (1560) and the Bishops' Bible.

The Geneva Bible has always been remembered as the attempted successor to the Great Bible that instead became a symbol of non-conformity under Elizabeth. The translation was a collaborative work of English theologians in exile under Mary Tudor. Miles Coverdale—the man who spearheaded the Great Bible—worked on this new translation along with William Whittingham, Anthony Gilby, and others. Some have claimed the Bible contained radical statements about overthrowing tyrants, but in fact the notes in the Geneva Bible were restrained for its time.

What was unmistakable, however, was the fact that the Geneva Bible was published in the same city as John Knox's *First Blast against the Monstrous Regiment of Women*—a bad attempt to justify overthrowing Mary since women, he argued, were forbidden to serve as head of government.[4] Elizabeth rose to the throne only months after Knox published the book, and she never forgave Knox or Geneva. When it was published the following year, already the Geneva Bible—as it came to be called—was marked as a dangerous translation.

In an effort to counteract the success of the Geneva Bible—its sales never lagged despite the awkward situation with Knox—the bishops of England created the Bishops' Bible. It was a wooden translation and never successful despite the support of church leaders. In time, the competing visions for England—Puritan and Anglican—saw their struggle in part as a decision over their distinctive Bible translations.

James I and the Bible

When James VI of Scotland was crowned James I of England, he inherited the messy relationship between Anglicans and Puritans.[5]

As it happens, he was just the man to help unite both sides toward a common task. What he was not, however, was a man who tolerated complaining—which he felt was the only language Puritans spoke. For most of his reign, even if James agreed with the Puritan side, if he sensed any disrespect from the Puritans, he would dig in his heels.

Why was James so belligerent against Puritan complaints? Part of the answer lies in his upbringing.

James was the infant king of Mary Queen of Scots, who made the foolish choice to plot her husband's murder before running off with her lover. This fatal choice paved the way for Scotland to become Protestant. Up to that time, Mary had been a staunch Catholic and had resisted all efforts to move Scotland toward Protestantism. With her betrayal of the king, she now forfeited both the crown and her life. She fled to England, seeking the support of her cousin, Elizabeth I, who had her put on house arrest immediately. The trouble for Elizabeth was that monarchs abhorred the idea that a king or queen could be executed. Only when Mary plotted to overthrow Elizabeth did she place her head on the block.

With his mother exiled, James was raised by the Protestant leaders now in control of Scotland. He was barely a year old when his father was murdered, and he never knew his mother. As a result, he never knew his mother's Catholic faith.

The Scottish leaders raised the boy essentially as property of the state. When he was old enough, he was assigned a tutor—and not just any tutor, but George Buchanan (1506–82). The son of a Highlander, Buchanan was a steady but severe man, the kind who would find a seat cushion a pointless luxury. He was also well educated, steeped in the study of humanism, and a thorough lover of the Bible.

You might say that Buchanan conducted an experiment on young James: If he taught the boy to be a godly king, would he submit to the Bible and avoid the pitfalls of his mother? Growing up in this environment, the future King James embraced the essential tenets of Reformed Protestantism. He also grew cold to the way Reformed theologians cajoled and browbeat political rulers. For example, one of Buchanan's more radical ideas was that a king could be punished for breaking the law—a nearly universal concept today, but an unpopular idea in the seventeenth century. James raised objections with his teacher over this, and not a few times they debated the matter openly. In the end, Buchanan did manage to make James a lover of the Bible. What he failed to do, however, was make James submit to his vision for a Reformed king.

Elizabeth I died in 1603, unmarried and therefore childless—the Virgin Queen of England. Quietly and quickly, James was chosen as the successor, since his great-grandmother had been Henry VIII's sister. James was thrilled, saying to his Scottish court that he was leaving a stone pillow for a feather bed. He set out for England, promising to return to Scotland every three years.

We are not sure of the reaction of the Puritans in England, but one can assume they were delighted. It was known that James had been a good king to the new Protestant church in Scotland, essentially allowing the pastors to govern themselves. To the Puritans, then, it seemed that the tables were now turned. Elizabeth had stifled their voice—though she truly resisted only the hot-blooded version of Puritanism. She had tolerated different opinions so long as those opinions did not stir up controversy. As James rode slowly for London, however, the Puritans assumed he was going to take their side. At last, they could clean out the stables.

Perhaps for this reason, the Puritan leaders hastened to get these issues in front of James. In April, before he even made it to London, a team of Puritan leaders rode to meet their new king. With them they had the Millenary Petition—named for the one thousand signatures on the document. The petition laid before James the issues that had created friction under Elizabeth, mostly on the subject of worship. Hat in hand, they offered the petition to James "neither as factious men . . . nor as schismatics." They knew some Anglican tongues would wag to James about Puritan rebellion, an easy flaw to exploit, since their grumbling about worship sounded treasonous. Now standing before James, still on the road to London, the Puritans tried to get in front of any rumors before he could hear them.[6]

James was not irked at having to start work before he was even crowned. Instead, he called for a session immediately with both parties, the Anglicans and the Puritans. That meeting was the Hampton Court Conference in 1604. Both sides felt the weight of the moment. What both sides did *not* anticipate, however, was to learn the real personality of their king: bracing, quick-witted, and unwilling to let either side rehash their old grievances. According to one account, James opened the meeting with a masterstroke to keep them off balance—bellowing at both sides as they tried to sit before he had settled himself. We should have some fun imagining them, Anglicans and Puritans, hovering halfway to their seats, wondering if they had awoken the king's wrath. Now, suddenly, James was Solomon, and the clergy were forced to argue over the baby.

Neither side won, neither lost. It is true that James mostly dismissed the Puritan complaints about worship. Too many assume that James simply hated his Puritan subjects. Instead, the list of requests in the Millenary Petition concerned, according to James, silly issues. He was not wrong on this point.

Essentially, the Puritan demands had grown and grown under Elizabeth. Not only did they want an end to bowing and wearing clerical robes, they also complained about wedding rings—superstitious metal that has no bearing on a marriage—and the practice of confirming children for communion. They even complained about the word *priest*.

James knew this for what it was: a haymaker punch against Anglicanism. He also knew, even if he agreed with some of their demands, he could not allow the Puritans to believe he would dance on their string. So he shut them down and told them they were fools. But James also gave the Anglicans a tongue lashing for ignoring the simple requests of their Puritan colleagues, bullying them into submission, and then gloating about the result. If they had listened more than once, James stressed, then maybe the situation would not have come to this.

Ultimately, James was embarrassed to inherit a divided Anglican church—and he wanted neither side to feel they had won at Hampton Court. In this, we glimpse some of James's policy on Puritanism: he decided to hold two apparent contradictions in tension. Like Elizabeth, he continued to stress the need for conformity to the pattern of Anglicanism, and yet, when reasonable, he would agree to allow more breathing room for those Puritans who felt the established church wounded their conscience. One may find this a bad gamble on peace, but it is also likely James was exercising good leadership—bending for the sake of those who needed it, not breaking for those who demanded it.

At some point the Puritan John Reynolds, a scholar from Oxford, suggested the idea of approving a new English translation of the Bible. James loved the idea. On the Bible, there was no division: both sides hewed to the Protestant understanding of the Word of God. The division between Anglicans and Puritans was simply over which translation—and more precisely, which theological notes—were superior. And even in theological notes, one had to look hard to find major variances in their theological positions.

James agreed to the new translation and ordered both sides to work on it. His only caveat was that he had two ground rules. First, he wanted no marginal notes at all. In fact, James wanted a Bible that was only a Bible, without commentary—a point a little ironic to have to enforce with Protestants, no matter their disagreements with each other. Second, James wanted the basis of the translation to begin with the Bishops' Bible—a hasty translation made during Elizabeth's reign—though he made it clear he wanted a *new* translation, not a repackaged version of the Elizabethan text. A new English Bible, and the Bible alone.

The First Edition

The work of those who created the KJV was rather less heroic than the story about James calling the Hampton Court Conference. We first should gain some perspective on what the KJV is. People today are used to talking about the King James "translation"—but the KJV was not a fresh *translation* into English. It was a *revision* of existing English copies along with a retooling of the translation to create something new. This is an important point that will be raised in later chapters, with the rise of modern English translations. As we saw in our previous chapter, nearly 90 percent of Tyndale's translation can still be found in our Bibles—meaning nearly all modern translations are also revisions. We should not overplay this point, but after the Tyndale and Coverdale Bibles, it was rare to have a translation team sit and go through the original text, word for word, writing down their new translation. The KJV committee did the same: they took existing English translations and their notes on the Hebrew and Greek and attempted to come up with the wording they felt was best.

From the start, it was clear that James's instructions to use the Bishops' Bible would not be enforced aggressively. Almost immediately, those included in the translation team used *all* existing copies of the Bible in English—including not only the Tyndale, Coverdale, and Great Bibles but also the Douai-Rheims translation by English Catholics.[7]

Since it would have been unwieldly to have everyone in a room together for each session, several teams worked in unison on the KJV. The use of different teams created some curious by-products. Perhaps the most striking is the language of the King James Bible. As much as we tend to think the KJV was a sample of spoken English in the 1600s, it actually was a rather archaic and formal wording by the standard of 1611.[8] This is not to say the wording was nonsense—as if we were to speak in Shakespearean English today—but the KJV sought to elevate the translation by adding a level of formalism. By contrast, the translation of William Tyndale, written almost a century before, sounds more contemporary. Mark 4:38, for example, in Tyndale says that Jesus was in the stern, though the KJV has gone with the more formal "he was in the hinder part of the ship." For Tyndale, Jesus always "sayde [said] unto them" rather than the KJV rendering that Jesus "saith unto them." This was not the typical pattern of speech in seventeenth-century England, and the language had not grown more formal since Tyndale. The translators of the KJV instead made it so.

We can only guess the reason, but it is likely the formalism was intended to elevate the grandeur of the translation—making it something of a throwback to the early years of the English Reformation—like someone today using an old-timey voice on the radio. Perhaps the translation team simply felt this was a better rendering. But even if we note the formalized style of the KJV, this did not detract from the quality of the work. The most cynical reader must admit there are places where the KJV translation is beautifully rendered. "There hath no temptation taken you but such as is common to man," reads 1 Corinthians 10:13, and many people have memorized verses like 1 John 1:9, "If we confess our sins, he is faithful and just to forgive us our sins, and to cleanse us from all unrighteousness."

One of the more noteworthy features of the KJV—one not typically found in Bible translations—is the way the translators rendered the same word in the original in a variety of ways in English. These decisions are not wrong, and even modern Bibles do this, but the problem was the various committees had different instincts. For example, the Greek word that means "straightaway" is taken in the KJV variously as "immediately," "anon," "by and by," "as soon as," "straightaway," and "shortly."[9] A bigger, theological problem may be created with their translation of Genesis 22:1, where "God did *tempt* Abraham"—though he was only tested. We can never be certain why they made this choice to translate Greek and Hebrew words in multiple ways, but the two best suggestions are: (1) different translators preferred different words, or (2) they simply wanted to expand the English usage to make the text read better.

Still other verses are simply mistranslated at points. The KJV is why we think of Joseph as having "a coat of many colours"—though the Hebrew simply means a coat with long sleeves. Numbers 23:22 wrongly mentions a unicorn, when the animal was a wild ox. Sometimes the translators mistook a person's name to be something else—any reader will be confused by Judges 15:19 since water gushed from "an hallow place that was in the jaw," when it actually gushed from a hollow place in Lehi (a Philistine encampment). They mistook the city of Bethel for the house of God, and Isaiah in the KJV refers to the existence of "satyrs" and "dragons" and mistakes wolves or hyenas for things called "wild beasts of the islands" (Isaiah 13:21–22). Many have memorized 1 Timothy 6:10 that love of money "is the root of all evil," when in fact love of money is a root of all kinds of evils—still a problem, but the Bible does not consider sin to be a problem of economics! The KJV translators were human, and they simply made some errors.

One of the more lasting changes the KJV made was in the choice of names in the Bible. The problem here, in part, is that the translation committees worked in tandem, not all together. As a result, some names are spelled differently throughout the Bible. We can simply list a few: Judah/Juda/Judas/Jude (all the same name), Golgotha/Calvary, Luke/Lucas, Elijah/Elias. Other times, the KJV inexplicably invents a name rather than follow the Hebrew. The man who led Israel after Moses is known in English as *Joshua*, when in fact his name is *Yeshua*—the same name as Jesus, obscuring an important connection between Old and New Testaments for English readers.[10] Perhaps most influential of all, the KJV took the intimate name for God—spelled *Yahweh* today in English—and made it *Jehovah*.

The list of problems like these from the 1611 edition could fill an entire chapter. Are these horrible stains on an important Bible? Certainly not. Anyone who has taken a course in Greek or

Hebrew can understand the challenge of translation. Languages are difficult, especially in a generation that was still making strides in biblical research. But as we shall see in our next chapter, these issues needed correction, and thus the KJV we have today is not the same as in 1611.

The KJV Legacy

Recent myths about the King James Bible will be covered in our final chapter. For now, we should end with a note about the legacy of the KJV, both in its own day and ever since. Other than the Luther Bible, no other Protestant translation has endured so long or shaped the minds and hearts of so many Christians as the KJV. Generations of Christians—including many today—if asked to quote from the Bible, have found the language of the KJV on their lips. Its verses have been read at more weddings, its lamentations said over more graves, than those of any other English translation. The story of how a Bible endured so long will be the subject of our next chapter.

Study Questions

1. Do you own a copy of the KJV? Who gave it to you?
2. Why do you think the Puritans were so upset about worship?
3. How should we view the KJV today?

Recommended Reading

Carson, D. A. *The King James Version Debate: A Plea for Realism*. Grand Rapids: Baker Academic, 1978.

Daniell, David. *The Bible in English*. New Haven: Yale Unversity Press, 2003.

McGrath, Alistair. *In the Beginning: The Story of the King James Bible and How It Changed a Nation, a Language, and a Culture*. New York: Doubleday, 2001.

Norton, David. *The King James Bible: A Short History from Tyndale to Today*. Cambridge: Cambridge University Press, 2011.

CHAPTER 12

THE MODERN BIBLE MOVEMENTS

Jonathan Swift was a man who would strike us as strange today. He wore powdered wigs—a fashion in the 1700s, since the white hair gave the status of wisdom—and wrote *Gulliver's Travels* as a satire of the English government. To make himself more lovable, he also complained about everyone's grammar. The English language, he felt, had suffered enormously in his day. Once a nation that had given the world Shakespeare, now the English spoke with little concern for proper grammar. If they did not act quickly, he said, they would trail behind Europe.

In 1712, Swift wrote his position on English grammar in a famous treatise, "*A Proposal for Correcting, Improving and Ascertaining the English Tongue*." Along with general complaints, the treatise also offered an opinion about the KJV. Swift wrote that, while his countrymen loved their English Bible, they had not appreciated how the KJV translators "were masters of an English style." Reading it in church weekly, he went on, is a solid defense for English, as it presents the highest standard of English, "especially to the common people."[1]

Such fulsome praise is typical for a seventeenth-century Englishman—proud of his nation, secure in both his nationalism and his Anglicanism, and optimistic about the future of Britain. For Swift, there was no distinction between the glories of the KJV and the supremacy of the Motherland. Everything, it seemed, was to support the establishment.

As we saw in our previous chapter, however, the KJV was not a perfect specimen in terms of biblical translation. If the KJV was a masterpiece, it was a masterpiece with the flaws that come from the shortcomings of being human. Bible scholars eventually saw the issues, but they did not wish to undermine the integrity of the KJV's accomplishments. England was also fully engrossed in westward expansion to the American colonies. But that expansion came at a cost. Once English Protestants began to arrive in the Colonies—along with other Protestant emigrants from countries like Germany, the Netherlands, and France—the ties to the Old World began to loosen. It would not be an overstatement to say that, along with political freedom, America became a land of a diverse and great number of Bibles.

This chapter will explore both the changes and influence of the KJV and the ways the Bible began to be used differently in the New World. Both factors contribute to the final period in our story of how we got our Bible.

The Bible of the Colonies

A century after Columbus discovered a new continent, these new lands were sought after by Protestant nations like England and the Netherlands. Catholic nations too began to expand almost immediately, especially into South America, but also into parts of the American Southwest. For most of the Reformation, however, Protestants were either disinterested or unable to attempt any serious western settlement until the time of Queen Elizabeth. The cost was prohibitive, and England was not always capable of footing the bill. It was also difficult to find people willing to relocate to a land that, to Europe, sounded like an impossible wilderness.

The first serious attempt during Elizabeth's reign was the Roanoke Colony, established in 1585. Not everyone remembers this, however, because of the tragic circumstances that befell the colony. We are still not sure what happened—but when ships arrived two years later, everyone from the colony had vanished. This is why Americans often think of Jamestown—established in 1607—as the first settlement. As the name suggests, it was named after King James of England.

Once Protestants were in the New World, the hope in England was that the Colonies would stem the tide of Catholic expansion around the world. Indeed, the taking of new lands by Europeans was almost an arms race between both sides of the Reformation— and King James supported those who wished to relocate. By 1700 there were 250,000 settlers in the Colonies, and by the 1770s there were as many as 2.1 million.

The settlers brought their Bibles with them, symbolically carrying the Reformation message of *sola scriptura* to the New World. But soon all sorts of Protestants from other countries, including Germany, France, and the Netherlands, arrived in the New World. Communities like the Moravians (from Germany) and the Dutch began to make their presence felt—and not just a few beleaguered French Huguenots escaped to the Colonies to avoid persecution. Before long, the Colonies had a welter of denominations, all with their own Bibles. The outcome was that by 1900, America had become a melting pot of denominations.

Many of the earliest settlers were broadly Puritan—at least

they shared the same concerns about the Anglican church. Not a few of them were accustomed to the Geneva Bible, especially during the early expansion, since the KJV was still new. But we must understand that almost immediately, groups that were neither Anglican nor Puritan began to arrive—like the Quakers and other Anabaptist communities. The habit of seeing the Colonies as merely a Puritan world is incomplete.

To take one example, the future state of Pennsylvania, when it began, looked almost nothing like Puritan New England. Over the course of the 1700s, it was a mixture of Quaker, Moravian, Congregational, and other groups. Many did not speak English natively, and so they cared little for the KJV Bible. Instead, they used their own Bibles. In the case of the Quakers, they even translated their own Bible in 1764. The translation was the work of Anthony Purver (1702–77). The quality was passable, though largely lifeless. Because it belonged to the Quakers, this new Bible was mocked by other Protestants. Rumors were invented that Purver had wrestled with difficult passages by practicing his Quaker belief in quietism, locking himself in his room, hoping divine inspiration would provide answers. Nonsense, of course, but the fact that such rumors were created shows us that something new was emerging in the New World: debates over Bible *translations* often reflected the struggle between Protestant *confessions*.

The Bible in the New World would no longer be controlled—at least not to the extent it was in Europe. Translations sprouted up everywhere, some of higher quality than others, though all served the needs of a denomination. Indeed, there are few denominations, even in our own day, that do not at some point adopt a certain Bible translation. This was not simply a theological squabble with the neighbors. Choosing a single Bible for a church or denomination creates a strong bond. Congregants can memorize the same verses and recite them in the same wording—and such bonds are deeply personal.

The King James (All Rights Reserved)

If the Bible would not be controlled in the New World, then this was especially true of the King James Version—historically one of the most controlled Bibles in history. For example, older laws for publishing had a few differences with modern laws. Publishers today are eager to protect their copyrights, and they will take steps in cases where their property is stolen. In previous centuries, however, it was impossible to enforce such a policy. In the sixteenth century, for example, with the Reformation creating a boom industry for printing, there was no such thing as piracy—at least how we define it today. Printers assumed their works might be copied, reprinted, and sold by other printers. And they did nothing to stop it. Even if you wanted to recoup money from a rogue printer—which would first require laws against piracy— there still were no means to watch markets in other cities, much less in other countries. Once you printed a book, you moved on to other projects.

The one country that worked against this trend, however, was England. The main reason was that England had the luxury of a centralized government. In fact, most of England's print shops were in London. The crown, therefore, could play an active role in governing local printing—just as we saw when William Tyndale was denied the right to publish an English Bible. Books typically needed royal approval, along with a stamp indicating the printer had received authorization. While some flouted these laws, in most circumstances, one could flip to the first page of a book to ensure the book was lawfully printed. By and large, these rules were enforced in cases where heretical texts were smuggled into the country—like when Henry wanted Lutheran books banned from England. But English authorities kept a watchful eye on the market, especially on production of the Bible.

The King James Bible was the most successful book to be regulated by the English crown. We should stress again, however, that printers holding the right to print the KJV is not the same as saying the Bible was given royal sanction. The KJV had no official status with the king, and it never would. The translation, of course, was *celebrated* by the crown and by the Anglican church, but no royal decree empowered the KJV.

The most important source of authority for the KJV, therefore, was its licensing. To control the market, it was necessary to control the text. In this case, the Barker family in London held the exclusive right to print Bibles. They had received this privilege from Elizabeth I in 1589, but their rights were extended under James I. Thus, with the new demand for the KJV, there was only one printer, one stockpile, to buy a copy. The only exceptions were the universities of Oxford and Cambridge, which were granted rights because of their role in education. But the Barker family initially was the only shop allowed to print the KJV.

This policy was wildly successful. From the time of the Tyndale Bible in the 1530s down to just before the KJV in 1611, by far the most popular text was the Tyndale version. The New Testament was especially popular and ran to forty editions in just over forty years. No other Bible could keep pace. Sales began to flag only after 1568, when pressure was put on churches to use the Anglican-approved Bishops' Bible and when the Geneva

Bible became the counter-Anglican choice for Puritans. From 1568 to 1610, these two Bibles were printed in ticktock patterns, in what can only be described as a printing race. Once the KJV was completed, however, it rapidly overtook nearly every other Bible printing in England. For example, in 1615 the KJV was given seven printing runs.[2]

As with anything in high demand, merchants soon found ways to make a profit. One method was to purchase copies of the KJV and then sell them in other cities or even in the Colonies. By the 1700s, this was done so often the king was forced to issue a decree that all Bibles must include its price on the title page. This managed only to slow Bible reselling, and clearly by 1700 the Bible was big business.

Perhaps the most diabolical way to exploit the system was to interpret the word *Bible* in its most precise definition—the bare text of the Bible. Printers, however, noticed that commentaries were not subject to regulation. So printers just added something that qualified as commentary and printed the KJV alongside it. At times, the notes were sloppy or little more than a few comments on each page. In a few instances, the pages were printed and, after they passed inspection, the commentary was sliced off so the printer could rebind the book.

The most successful strategy was the invention of the Family Bible—a massive tome with pages to record births, deaths, and other moments. This allowed families to display their Bible in their home, and soon enough craftsmen were selling special furniture for Family Bibles. The Family Bible was both Scripture and heirloom in one package.

But the movement that forever broke the KJV free of regulation was the American Revolution. The unshackling of the Colonies from England meant that local printers could ignore regulations. Still, it is curious that the KJV continued to be a fixture in the new United States—not the only Bible, but a favorite choice for many churches. In time, most began to see the printing of the KJV as something they *took back* from England. In 1777, only a matter of months after the Declaration of Independence, the newly established Congress debated whether to fund a printing of the KJV—not a topic one would think vital for a young nation. But the point is that the KJV endured in America as a symbol of overcoming British tyranny. The KJV therefore became part of the fabric of American churches.

The Church's One but Varied Foundation

One of the idiosyncratic features of American Protestantism is the sheer number of denominations. In nearly every city, it is normal to drive past dozens of different Protestant churches—and increasingly in the last 150 years, Catholic and Orthodox churches. The fact is, this is not the norm for much of the world, especially in the West, where historically nations have trended toward one or two denominations. By contrast, many regular church attenders in America have in their lifetime joined more than one denomination.

The story of the Bible has given us a clue as to how these various churches will interact. Simply put, if you were to attend three different churches in America, you might find three different Bibles in English. There also have arisen Bible societies, translation networks, and a host of Protestant movements that, while sharing the same belief in the authority of the Bible, do not share a commitment to a single translation. This is a contrast to the older European tradition of the Reformation, where typically one translation tended to draw all the churches together, as each used the same Bible in worship. It is uniquely American to believe that the Bible alone is our foundation—yet churches cannot agree *which* Bible is the version that best embodies this doctrine.

One way to understand this tension is to see how the Bible becomes wrapped up in the language of individual freedom. After the American Revolution, the church began to take on the same principles of democracy and personal liberty that shaped the new nation. In fact, historians have called this the *democratization* of the church—a time when the authority of pastors and church leaders began to atrophy. In time, churches could no longer control which Bible must be used by their members. Even today, denominations rarely mandate which version must be read in the pulpit, much less in the pew.

American individualism also drove a number of new translations in the eighteenth and nineteenth centuries. Some of these translations were the work of only one translator. We already mentioned the Quaker Bible by Anthony Purver. To this list we can add the *Self-Interpreting Bible* (1792)—a useful Bible if teachers or pastors are unavailable. The *Darby Bible* (complete edition, 1890) focused on issues of translation John Nelson Darby felt needed correction.

So the challenge of American churches was to encourage one version of the Bible without coercing members. Some denominations were helped by having a dynamic founder—such as the Methodist Church had in John Wesley. His translation, with notes on the New Testament, was published in 1755. This version has always avoided the word *translation*, as it is a revision of the KJV according to Wesley's theological understanding of the Bible's wording. While at Oxford before his missionary journeys began, Wesley taught Greek, so he was certainly qualified for the task. The result was a Bible that fit his theology without overly bending the text's original meaning. For example, he changed the word *shall* to *will*, which one scholar argues was so Wesley could avoid an unnecessary conclusion about predestination.[3] Wesley's chief concern, however, was to make the KJV more accessible to those he converted on his journeys—uneducated folks with little knowledge of the Bible and no desire to trudge through the now archaic language of the KJV.

One translation that stands out in this period is *The Holy Bible: Containing the Old and New Testaments; Translated Literally from the Original Tongues*,[4] published in 1876. This was the first translation of the entire Bible by a woman. Julia E. Smith Parker loved studying biblical languages—her father had been a pastor of a Congregational church in Connecticut—and took up the translation project, it seems, as a labor of love. She only agreed to have the Bible published in 1876—when she was eighty-four years old, twenty-one years after she had finished the work. Parker was lovably feisty, saying once she never sought help from Bible scholars because she didn't think she needed it. She had a clear exegetical standard in her translation. Although it does not make for the best English translation, her method was to be thoroughly consistent in her translations. A word in the original must *always* be translated the same—not with a synonym. Verb tenses must *always* work the same way. Only in nineteenth-century America does one find such plucky individualism associated with Bible translation.

But the Bible was now free of restrictions, and that was a good thing. It made American Protestants nimble, able to adapt to the demand without legal restrictions. Still, if older English Bibles, such as the KJV, were considered unworthy, what would be a better alternative? The answer came with a new word that would forever be associated with Bible translations: *literal*.

In 1862, there was *Young's Literal Translation*—the earliest example we have found of a Bible version using this word. It was the work of Robert Young, who also made a popular concordance of the Bible. The translation has always raised eyebrows, since Young clearly took issue with other versions of the Bible. The preface barked about how the Bible must be translated perfectly from the original. He went on to cite how existing Bibles took a present-tense verb and translated it in the past tense or the opposite, or how an imperative would be used for a subjunctive, a verb for a noun, or a noun for a verb. He concluded:

> It is clear that verbal inspiration is as much overlooked as if it had no existence.
> THE WORD OF GOD IS MADE VOID BY THE TRADITIONS OF MEN.[5]

Never before had a Bible translation been based on such naked, foaming anger. Also new was the claim that any leeway on verb tenses was the result of Satan's influence.

Publishers ever since have used the word *literal* to describe new translations, but the word now is a synonym for *true* or *faithful*. But as we have noted throughout this book, languages always have idioms, expressions, and phrases that make no sense when translated word for word into another language. As we shall see in our next chapter, this desire to get to a better, more accurate translation will be one of the hallmarks of twentieth-century Bibles.

Bible Translation as Missions

One final word can be said about the Bible in America. Until the nineteenth century, the need for Bibles was always grounded in the life of the church. Bibles were for the discipleship and training of new Christians.

The nineteenth century, however, saw the rise of new movements that strove to use the Bible for Christian missions and evangelism. This focus on unreached people created new urgency for churches to send missionaries trained in Bible translation. It also inspired evangelists at home who shared their faith with their neighbors. Both of these factors drove a new idea: the Bible can be used as a tool for evangelism.

But if the Bible was a tool for evangelism and mission, it soon became necessary to make the Bible simpler as a first step to hearing the gospel. In our day, this can be seen in paraphrased Bibles—such as *The Message* by Eugene Peterson—written in plain language, attempting to communicate the Word through general thoughts.

The other felt need was to increase biblical literacy itself. Churches and seminaries both continue to strategize how to help lay Christians undersand the basics of the Bible. One can no longer assume that men and women today have ever opened a Bible.

Over the last two centuries, the Bible has transitioned from being a tool for *discipleship* to a tool for *conversion*. This is an explosive idea, but one that shapes the instincts of those who make translations.

The first Bible translated for missions work goes back to the late 1600s and the work of John Eliot. When he came to the Colonies, Eliot settled in the Roxbury area of Boston, where he served as pastor of the First Church in Roxbury. He founded the Roxbury Latin School in 1645, today the oldest school in continuous operation in North America.[6]

Eliot was inspired to reach Native Americans in the region

of the Massachusetts Bay Colony—the Massachusett tribe. The main obstacle that prevented Eliot from evangelizing members of the tribe was the language barrier. He soon found help from a young member of the tribe named Cockenoe who had learned to speak English after he was captured in a war over control of trade and became a servant to an Englishman. The two fumbled through the words—Cockenoe knowing both English and the Algonquin language. Eliot translated the Lord's Prayer and the Ten Commandments after creating the first written system for the tribe's language.

The Massachusett spoke Natick, a dialect of the Algonquin language. After fourteen years of toil, Eliot completed a translation of the Geneva Bible into Natick in 1663. Today it is known as the *Eliot Indian Bible*, but the actual title page reads *Mamusse Wunneetupanatamwe Up-Biblum God*.[7] It was the first Bible printed in the New World. It was also the first Bible of modern missions, made for evangelism, translated by a non-native speaker. This had not happened in nearly seven-hundred years, when some of the first Anglo-Saxon Bibles were translated by Christian missionaries.

Today Eliot is largely forgotten, but he was a hero to Christians in the Colonies and is commemorated in the Episcopal liturgy on May 21. The Massachusett honor his legacy too as the man who gave them a written language.

We will have more to say on the Bible and modern missions in our next chapter, but a conclusion is helpful now. John Eliot's work to make a Bible for the Massachusett tribe exemplifies the flexibility of Bible translation in the New World while also reaffirming the basic commitment to the Word shared by Protestants since the Reformation. Eliot was the first to do this in the context of missionary work, but he would not be the last. In the twentieth century, the expansion of missionary work around the globe—especially to unreached people—was carried along by translation of the Bible into the mother tongues of people groups. In 1800, the Bible had been translated into 70 languages. By 1900 there were 500 languages with Bible translations, and by 1925 there were 835.

Study Questions

1. Do you think the Bible is mostly for discipleship or mostly for missions? Or can it be both?
2. Do you think there is a problem with having a variety of translations of the Bible? Do you wish there was only one? Explain.
3. Was anything wrong with the KJV being controlled for printing before the American Revolution? Should the Bible simply be copyright free?

Recommended Reading

Campbell, Gordon. *Bible: The Story of the King James Version, 1611–2011.* Oxford: Oxford University Press, 2010.

Noll, Mark. *In the Beginning Was the Word: The Bible in American Public Life, 1492–1783.* Oxford: Oxford University Press, 2015.

THE BIBLE TODAY—
AND TOMORROW

The story of the Bible is a story of change. First in Hebrew, then Greek and Latin—from hand-copied papyrus sheets to the Gutenberg press. The Bible has been a tool for conformity and a firebrand in the hand of reformers. It has been tightly controlled and smuggled into countries under the noses of government officials. But in all these contexts, it is the Word of God.

We come now to the final stage in the story—the twentieth century (and now the twenty-first century). The number of Bible translations around the world has increased rapidly over the last century. Today there are new efforts to translate the Bible into even more languages. There is simply no way to do justice to all of the wonderful nooks and crannies of this recent history. So we will focus on a few cases of the most influential changes to the Bible in the modern world.

Two areas, in particular, deserve our attention. First is the rise of societies and parachurch organizations founded on the vision to see the Bible made available around the world. The second area involves new translations—those that have tried but not managed to unseat the KJV from its place as the Bible most Christians read on a regular basis.

The Bible Societies

In our previous chapter, we discussed how the KJV was controlled by the English crown at first and later (along with other versions) became free of restrictions in the New World. This allowed printers, translators, and editors to use this version for their own ends. We also looked briefly at how the Bible became a tool for missionary work. What we must explore now is how the passion for affordable Bibles and the passion for new translations worked together in the creation of Bible societies.

It can be easy to overlook the numerous Bible societies that have toiled to provide Bibles for the modern world. Modern Bible societies have achieved a staggering level of success in their printing operations—all on the cheap. These groups drove down the price of Bibles—and in the case of Gideons International, Bibles were and are given away free of charge. The legacy of these societies is not only in the printing of millions of Bibles but also, in our time, in the number of Bible translations available online that are free of charge.

The man who helped launch Bible societies in the modern world was John Thornton—an evangelical Anglican and a philanthropist who later served as director of the Bank of England. Seldom has a man been so free with his wealth—traveling throughout England for business and donating to churches and ministries no matter their affiliation, later helping fund the establishment of Dartmouth College. Each year he gave away at least half of his earnings. One of the ministries he supported was the formation of the Bible Society in 1779, led by two lay Methodist ministers, John Davie and George Cussons.[1]

Almost at once, other societies sprouted up in both Britain

and the United States. The most influential society in Britain was the British and Foreign Bible Society, founded in 1804. Leading voices in British evangelicalism were part of its founding—William Wilberforce, in particular—and it focused on spreading the Bible only to areas without Bibles, or where the cost was too great for many to purchase a Bible. The inspiration for the society, in part, came from stories of the lack of Bibles in the Welsh language, and the vision expanded to take on the need for Bibles around the world. The society has endured to this day, and in the latter half of the twentieth century, it was distributing more than 150 million copies annually.

This British and Foreign Bible Society also played an important role in modern Bibles when it made the decision to remove the Apocrypha from the translations.[2] This may sound odd, since almost all English Bibles today do not have the Apocrypha. But long after the Reformation, Protestant Bibles continued to be published with the Apocrypha. Although Protestant traditions did not see the Apocrypha as canonical, it continued to be printed in Bibles. It not only was printed in the KJV but also appeared in the Geneva Bible for most of its early history. Ironically, Protestants never cite the Apocrypha as Scripture or write commentaries on these books. For years the Apocrypha was hidden in plain sight.

In the 1820s, the British and Foreign Bible Society was plunged into controversy when some of its members protested the inclusion of the Apocrypha in their edition of the Bible. In fact, the controversy split the society, and animosity toward the Apocrypha reached a level not seen in previous centuries. The issue arose, however, because of the success of the society in distributing Bibles in largely Catholic countries. While lay Protestants always understood the Apocrypha was not part of the Old Testament canon, many in the society wanted the Bible to be more visibly Protestant. In the end, the British and Foreign Bible Society removed the Apocrypha, and by the twentieth century, most Protestant Bibles would follow suit.

In America, societies for the Bible also flourished. The American Bible Society was formed in 1816—later known for its Good News Translation—and would become one of the most fruitful Bible distribution societies in the last century. Its mission was to supply Bibles to the poor—an ever-increasing problem in the nineteenth century—and it did so by leaps and bounds. The society mainly succeeded through efforts to raise donations to offset the price of each Bible. Shortly after the society was founded, it could offer the New Testament for just ninety cents by today's standards, while a full Bible was nine dollars.[3] According to the society's records, six-million copies of the Bible were distributed in its first three decades, and by 1900 the number had jumped to more than thirty-five million.

In many ways, the American Bible Society's influence on other Bible societies was stronger than some may realize. Before the nineteenth and twentieth centuries, Bible translation and printing were nearly always lodged within a denomination or theological tradition—save those early examples of translations by individuals in the 1700s. Printers in the States pursued the KJV without the restrictions of official licensing. But what Bible societies achieved is a further liberation of the Bible, moving publication and distribution into a wider, multidenominational framework. One today can hardly think of the Bible—at least the biblical text—as being anything but unrestricted, unlimited, and free.

The New Contenders

In 1885, a new Bible was published at Oxford known as the Revised Version, or RV.[4] Perhaps unknowingly, the committee that translated this new Bible had stumbled into a public-relations nightmare. Not a few people grabbed pitchforks against the men who dared revise the KJV.

Nearly all the fury came from the United States, especially from the emerging Fundamentalist movement. Two main factors contributed to the anger. First, there were suspicions about the source of the translation—based mostly on a fear of scholarship. Many evangelicals had grown sour to education, not only through clashes of worldview with the rise of liberalism but also because education gradually was seen as a detriment to spiritual health. Second, the KJV was simply the Bible many were comfortable reading. More importantly, the RV was offered as more than a revision—it was said to be an improvement on the KJV, using older Greek texts than those available in the Reformation.

As we mentioned in the introduction, the issue of textual criticism is important for modern Bible translation. Throughout the seventeenth and eighteenth centuries, new Greek texts were discovered that exposed the weaknesses of the original Greek text used, not only for the KJV but for other Protestant Bibles. The crucial development behind the RV (and all later English Bibles) was the publication by Westcott and Hort—both serving on the original RV translation teams—of a critical Greek New Testament (1881). This text was a landmark work, both collecting the advances in biblical studies until that point and offering new paths for research. Westcott and Hort allowed scholars to consider any debatable issues themselves since their Greek New Testament included critical notes designed to show their rationale for each verse.

Scholars had also expanded their knowledge of Greek and Hebrew idioms and knew better how to translate some of those places where the KJV had made a mistake. If anything, the desire to correct these problems came from the stodgy old Protestant belief that everything must be based on the Bible. So if our Bibles were translated using twelfth-century copies of Byzantine texts with several defects, then holding tight to the the KJV for the sake of these verses could be based only on hysteria and a crass appeal to tradition. More on these issues in a moment.

We can offer some sympathy for lay Christians who were stunned by the claims of the RV. Not all reactions to the RV were based on fearmongering, but on a desire to hold on to their tattered and worn Bibles. In many homes, the KJV had been the family Bible for generations—read at the dinner table, quoted in wedding vows, and recited at ordination services. The large Family Bibles we discussed in our previous chapter had births, deaths, anniversaries, and other milestones recorded on their pages. Even without these social connections to the KJV, many people had simply read and memorized their Bibles in the language of the KJV. To hear that the KJV was not only flawed but based on Greek manuscripts that were imperfect seemed almost slanderous to many Christian ears. And woe to anyone who attacked the KJV, the perfect translation in the English language.

Still, as we saw in previous chapters, the KJV was not without its problems. To be fair, the discoveries of older Greek manuscripts had materially changed only a handful of texts. Perhaps the new English style of the RV, much different from the KJV, made the distinction more severe.

But setting aside the Greek issues, the KJV translation quality itself was weak in places. The most glaring issue for most readers, however, was the archaic language of the KJV, which was already a problem in the eighteenth century, now more so as the twentieth century drew near.

Over the years, the gaffes and smaller flaws in the KJV had been tidied, often during a new print run. So there had always been an implicit admission of the need for improvement to the translation—never stated with malice, but admitted by nearly everyone. The fervent clutch of American readers who would not let go of the older KJV was the result of an immediate reaction against the RV and all other English translations.

The RV was the work of fifty-four scholars, the most notable of whom were J. B. Lightfoot, B. F. Westcott, and F. J. A. Hort—as well as Philip Schaff and others from America. The choice of those who served on the teams was not accidental. Each was a scholar of either the Bible or theology, and they represented a range of denominations, since the project helped many Protestant denominations. This was no small amount of work either, as the New Testament committee met for eleven years and the Old Testament committee for fifteen years.[5] The New Testament was completed and published in 1881, followed by the entire Bible in 1885.

Scholars are always eager for debate—pinching at a crumb and forgetting the feast—and in a demonstration of this, the British and American translation teams did not always agree on specific points in the translation. The British side carried the day, but they accommodated the American team by printing their opinions as an appendix. Unmoved by this gesture, the American team continued to work on their version of the translation—and fourteen years later, in 1901, the American group released their translation, the American Standard Version (ASV), today known simply as the Standard Version.[6] The two versions are nearly identical, save those areas where they quarreled. Overall, the British version was more elegant in its language, and the ASV was until recently considered a slightly clunkier, more wooden translation.

Two versions from one translation effort, divided between British and American versions. Some readers were unsettled, since cherished verses from the KJV now read differently—or worse, favorite verses were said to be corruptions of the Bible. The RV and ASV, as a result, were received poorly, especially in the States. The RV was even discussed in one of Joseph McCarthy's Senate hearings on Communism in 1953, while seven years later a note was sent to the US Navy Reserves, warning them of possible Communist influences on the new Bible. The KJV may not have been perfect, but at least we knew the King James was not an advocate for Communism. (Neither were the RV translators, in fact.)

Still, the door was now open to this sort of criticism. Bible translators knew they had to work harder to communicate the trustworthiness of their new translations if they were going to gain new readers. A translation is worth very little if it is appreciated by only a handful of scholars.

Following the Great Depression and two World Wars, the Revised Standard Version (RSV) was published in 1952. This version is the heir of both the ASV and RV, though it made strides in terms of readability. It was clear that this version was necessary after the backlash against the earlier translations. Regarding the quality of its English, the RSV trounced the two previous versions. The importance of this cannot be overstated, since subsequent English translations rise or fall, not on the basis of their textual criticism but on the degree to which Christians enjoy reading them. Again, the audience was comprised of lay Christians, and few things vex Bible readers more than delivering the Word of God in lifeless prose. Further strides in the RSV occurred in the 1970s when a new committee was gathered. The result of their efforts was the 1989 edition of what was called the New Revised Standard Version (NRSV), which is still sold today.

The last version in this family of translations is the New American Standard Bible (NASB)—a translation that altered the original ASV, though the two are hardly even related in their final form. The NASB was funded by the Lockman Foundation in California, which released a complete Bible in 1973. This version may have drawn some wisdom from the backlash against the RV. The most important feature of the NASB has always been its stress that it is the *most literal* translation in history—that statement is often embossed on the cover. The mission statement also declares that it will not focus attention on its translators since the glory of God's Word should focus on Christ, not scholars. These are good ways to win over a hostile crowd.

Of these translations, the only one to take much of the market before 1980 was the last one, the NASB. Each version in this translation family weathered the criticisms of KJV users. Critics combed through each translation, looking for hints of liberalism or weak rendering of the original languages. Few Bible versions can hold up to such scrutiny, especially when an ax is ready to chop. But this family of Bibles has endured.

New Translations, Similar Goals

The most important factor in all modern Bibles is how they approach the process of translation, an issue we mentioned in the introduction. Are they translated word for word or by dynamic equivalent? Most modern translations use a word-for-word approach. The NASB did this and stressed the word *literal* in its marketing.

The first Bible to attempt a dynamic equivalent translation on a large scale was the New English Bible (1970). Published jointly by Oxford and Cambridge, the translation was spearheaded by C. H. Dodd, an influential critical scholar from the University of Cambridge. The method was bold, but the result was controversial. First, it placed the Apocrypha back with the Bible—the idea being to reach the broadest audience. Second, it radically altered many verses. Not everyone liked the choices made by Dodd and the translators. For example, Genesis 1:1 now read:

> In the beginning of creation, when God made heaven and earth . . . a mighty wind swept over the surface of the water.

Not only is the time of creation rendered vague, but God's Spirit is downgraded to simply an act of nature. (The Hebrew word can mean either "spirit" or "wind," but this translation decision was seen as a direct shot at traditional theology.)

The most popular translation that takes a moderately dynamic-equivalent approach is the New International Version (NIV)[7]—today the bestselling Bible in the English-speaking world. The NIV's approach was not necessarily new, although it was not a typical method for Protestant Bibles, and evangelicals had tended to resist anything that wasn't word for word. At the time, many believed the risk was too high for scholars to inject their own ideas into the text and confuse the original meaning. By the 1960s, however, quite a few English Bibles were being sold. Each claimed to translate the Bible using a word-for-word method.

Some scholars believed the time was ripe to explore a blended approach that used dynamic equivalence in moderation. After all, *stuffy* and *lifeless* were not descriptors for a proper translation of the Bible.

The original committee was made up of leading scholars from a generation ago, all from a number of Protestant denominations, among them Edmund Clowney, Burton Goddard, and Charles Ryrie. In 1965, when work began on the NIV, the translation team wanted to embrace readability without sacrificing accuracy. About a hundred scholars worked on the NIV for ten years.

The result was a wild success—at least when compared with all versions made until that point. The New Testament came out in 1973, with two revisions issued in 1978 and 1984. The full Bible was released in 1978 and has been revised several times since. The NIV has not been without controversy, though in this case, the judgment is mostly from pastors and scholars. At times, critics claim the translation committees of the NIV inject too much bias into their translation, though it is hard to imagine any modern translation avoiding this critique. Others took issue with the TNIV—a version of the NIV published in 2005 that used gender-inclusive (or neutral) language. So instead of God making man, the TNIV says he created human beings. Jesus no longer tells the peacemakers they will be "*sons*" of God but "*children*" of God (though the KJV also rendered this passage as "*children*"). The charge here was that some of the wording of the New Testament was perhaps altered for the sake of modern English usage—and, for some, this made it seem as if the Word was made to conform to our culture. Any translation that gives attention to thought-for-thought meaning risks such criticism.

The Bible for Today

A final word about recent translations and the future of our Bible. The first thing we must note is that the English Bible today is still being translated not only in English but also into new languages around the world. Christains sometimes wonder if there are too many Bibles on the market. To give a better perspective on that concern, we'll divide English Bibles into five families:[8]

- *Bibles in the King James family.* These include not only the KJV but the New King James Version (NKJV) as well as many others. They include simple revisions to fix small errors, significant corrections or revisions, and even some more recent versions that seek to *restore* elements from 1611.
- *Bibles in the RV family.* These Bibles include those discussed already as well as newer translations, such as the English Standard Version (ESV) and New English versions. Several paraphrases—such as the Living Bible and its successor the New Living Translation (NLT)— are based on the ASV. So too is the Amplified Bible.
- *Bibles in the NIV family.* These include all the editions of the NIV as well as a sizable number of paraphrases and simplified versions, such as The Message.
- *Bibles that stand alone.* These are done by individuals, often for personal reasons, or for their church or denomination. There are a number of these, such as the Holman Christian Standard Bible.
- *New Vernacular Catholic Bibles.* For our study, we have not been able to tell this story, but new Catholic Bibles

should not be ignored. The rule that demanded Catholics use the Vulgate was relaxed at Vatican II. Around that time (and ever since), English versions of the Bible have been developed for Catholic readers. These include the Jerusalem Bible (JB), the New American Bible (NAB), the New Catholic Bible, and Bibles that borrow from one of the Protestant families, such as the Catholic edition of the New Living Translation, published in 2017.

In other words, there are not as many Bibles as we might think when we see them on bookshelves. There are four Protestant English families, and within each, there have been successful and unsuccessful translations. But each family continues to generate new interest and new ideas.

The history of the Bible in modern times has opened a world of access to the Bible impossible to believe in earlier centuries. Now that access to the Scriptures is available to the masses—free of charge, on both web-based and mobile applications—the Bible continues to be the foundation for millions of Christians, not only in the West but around the globe.

Study Questions

1. Do you think a Bible should be word for word or thought for thought in its translation? Why?
2. Should new English Bible translations focus on making the Bible conform to modern English—using things like gender-inclusive language, modern expressions, and English style? Why or why not?

3. Do you own or read a paraphrase version of the Bible? What are your thoughts on these translations?

Recommended Reading

Fee, Gordon, and Mark Strauss. *How to Choose a Translation for All Its Worth: A Guide to Understanding and Using Bible Versions.* Grand Rapids: Zondervan, 2007.

Köstenberger, Andreas J., and David A. Croteau. *Which Bible Translation Should I Use? A Comparison of Four Major Recent Versions.* Nashville: B&H, 2012.

NOTES

Foreword

1. For more on the history of the doctrine of Scripture, see Justin S. Holcomb, ed., *Christian Theologies of Scripture: A Comparative Introduction* (New York: New York University Press, 2006).
2. This phrase is from Article VI of the Thirty-Nine Articles. For more on the Thirty-Nine Articles, see Justin S. Holcomb, *Know the Creeds and Councils* (Grand Rapids: Zondervan, 2014), 123–30.

Chapter 1: Who's on First

1. This is a brief adaptation. The full routine can be seen in Jean Yarbrough, dir., *The Naughty Nineties* (Universal City, CA: Universal Pictures, 1945).
2. "The Best of the Century," Time.com, December 26, 1999, http://content. time.com/time/magazine/article/0,9171,36533,00.html.
3. A good book on this subject that looks at each biblical book or unit of books is Gordon D. Fee and Douglas Stuart, *How to Read the Bible for All Its Worth*, 4th ed. (Grand Rapids: Zondervan, 2014).
4. The riddle is described in detail in Frans van Liere, *An Introduction to the Medieval Bible* (Cambridge: Cambridge University Press, 2014), 19–20.
5. This likely comes from the Hebrew, where "before" is לִפְנֵי, which is literally "to the face up."
6. The KJV and ESV are the only two that keep it "send . . . before thy [ESV: your] face."
7. Later debates at times raise *new* disputes over a book that had always been received as canonical.
8. Charles E. Hill, *Who Chose the Gospels? Probing the Great Gospel Conspiracy* (Oxford: Oxford University Press, 2010).

Chapter 2: The Old Testament

1. The psalm is arranged as an acrostic, with each line beginning with the next letter in the Hebrew alphabet. Without these last two verses, the order was interrupted at the letter *nun*, similar to our letter N.
2. A great survey of the Pentateuch is T. Desmond Alexander, *From Paradise to the Promised Land: An Introduction to the Pentateuch* (Grand Rapids: Baker Academic, 2012). See also Victor Hamilton, *Handbook on the Pentateuch* (Grand Rapids: Baker Academic, 2015).
3. There is also an Aramaic term in Gen 31:47—though Aramaic was not the language Moses spoke.
4. A good survey is Robert Chisholm, *Handbook on the Prophets* (Grand Rapids: Baker Academic, 2009).

5. Since *hagiography* today means either the life of a saint or a poor example of historical whitewashing of the past, we usually refrain from using this word for the Writings.
6. The fourth book in the wisdom literature is Ecclesiastes, which is in the second division of the Jewish ordering.
7. See Matt 5:17; 7:12; 11:13; 22:40; Luke 16:16; 24:44; John 1:45; Acts 13:15; 24:14; 28:23; Rom 3:21.
8. *Against Apion* 1.42. The translation is taken from John M. G. Barclay, *Against Apion*, vol. 10 of *Flavius Josephus: Translation and Commentary*, ed. Steve Mason (Leiden: Brill, 2006), 29. See also Stephen G. Dempster, "The Old Testament Canon, Josephus, and Cognitive Environment," in *The Enduring Authority of the Christian Scriptures*, ed. D. A. Carson (Grand Rapids: Eerdmans, 2016), 321–61.

Chapter 3: The Septuagint and the Apocrypha

1. This is also true of other language groups in the ancient world.
2. The Greeks also took on Eastern customs whenever they wanted.
3. Background can be found in Karen Jobes and Moisés Silva, *Invitation to the Septuagint*, 2nd ed. (Grand Rapids: Baker Academic, 2015), 10–112.
4. We will see this later in this book, in the stories of the Vulgate and KJV, both of which have attached to them stories of providential care in their formation.
5. The Septuagint also refers to the older Greek translation, and we distinguish it from other Greek versions later in history that attempted to improve the quality of the older translation. On the variety of manuscripts, see Ernst Würthwein, *The Text of the Old Testament: An Introduction to the Biblia Hebraica* (Grand Rapids: Eerdmans, 2014), 50–78.
6. M. F. Wiles, "Origen as Bible Scholar," in *From the Beginnings to Jerome*, vol. 1 of *The Cambridge History of the Bible*, ed. P. R. Ackroyd and C. F. Evans (Cambridge: Cambridge University Press, 1970), 457 (Origen, *Comm. in Matt.* 15.14).

Chapter 4: The New Testament

1. It is not clear if "like a dove" refers to the *manner* of the Spirit's descent or if there was a manifestation that *looked* like a dove. Most artistic depictions of this scene paint a physical dove.
2. The language of "three persons" was established at the Council of Nicaea in AD 325. On this, see Donald Fairbairn and Ryan Reeves, *The Story of Creeds and Confessions* (Grand Rapids: Baker Academic, forthcoming).
3. Yoma 9b.
4. It also explains the role of John the Baptist as the last prophet.
5. For this language in Old Testament prophecies against Israel before the exile, cf. Jer 4:4; Ezek 36:26–28. Much of this, of course, is echoing Deut 30:6.
6. *Syn* = together, *opsis* = view.

Chapter 5: The Earliest Christians

1. The entire discussion can be found at *Ecclesiastical History*, 3.25.3–5.

2. A view examined in Charles E. Hill, *The Johannine Corpus in the Early Church* (Oxford: Oxford University Press, 2004).
3. *Against Apion* 1.37–43 (Barclay, 28–32).
4. *Exhortation to the Greeks* 13 (*The Ante-Nicene Fathers*, ed. A. Roberts and J. Donaldson, 10 vols. [1885–87; repr., Peabody, MA: Hendrickson, 1994]), 1:279.
5. Charles Hill, *Who Chose the Gospels? Probing the Great Gospel Conspiracy* (Oxford: Oxford University Press, 2012).
6. One of us has defended the importance of the Muratorian Fragment in C. E. Hill, "The Debate over the Muratorion Fragment and the Development of the Canon," *Westminster Theological Journal* 57.2 (Fall 1995): 437–52.

Chapter 6: The Vulgate

1. The only authoritative biography is J. N. D. Kelly, *Jerome: His Life, Writings, and Controversies* (Peabody, MA: Hendrickson, 1998).
2. A similar discussion and overview can be found in Christopher de Hamel, *The Book: A History of the Bible* (London: Phaidon, 2001), 14.
3. H. F. D. Sparks, "Jerome as Bible Scholar," in *From the Beginnings to Jerome*, vol. 1 of *The Cambridge History of the Bible*, ed. P. R. Ackroyd and C. F. Evans (Cambridge: Cambridge University Press, 1970), 511 (Jerome, *Letters* 22.30).
4. These hermit years are where some of the legends of his life come from—for example, the story of Jerome pulling a thorn from a lion's paw.
5. For more on Constantinople and the Nicene Creed, see Fairbairn and Reeves, *Story of Creeds and Confessions*.
6. This and other heresies—and the councils that met to settle them—are discussed in Justin Holcomb, *Know the Heretics* (Grand Rapids: Zondervan, 2014); idem, *Know the Creeds and Councils* (Grand Rapids: Zondervan, 2014).
7. Much like we transliterate *Yahweh* in English.
8. *On Christian Doctrine* 2.8; *The City of God* 18.20.
9. De Hamel, *Book*, 25. On the evidence left behind in manuscript form, the entirety of the first chapter is excellent.

Chapter 7: The Medieval Bible

1. De Hamel, *Book*, 27–28. De Hamel's book is especially good on the medieval period.
2. Ibid., 34.
3. A famous example is Codex Amiatinus (A), which has recently returned to Jarrow.
4. Estimations about animals and other materials, as well as the time needed for production, can be found in de Hamel, *Book*, 82.

Chapter 9: The Bible and the Reformation

1. *Sola scriptura* literally means "*by Scripture alone*," not that Protestants only read Scripture or do not have other, lesser authorities, such as confessions. See Carl Trueman, *The Creedal Imperative* (Wheaton, IL: Crossway, 2012). For a historically accurate treatment of Scripture alone, see Matthew

Barrett, *God's Word Alone—The Authority of Scripture* (Grand Rapids: Zondervan, 2016).
2. Therefore, many historians do not capitalize *humanism* in their writing, though textbooks often do.
3. *Ad fontes* means "*to the fount or fountain*," meaning back to the wellspring of the early centuries of the church.
4. An imperial diet was the place where business was conducted by the Holy Roman Empire, though it moved to different cities—in this case, the city of Worms.

Chapter 10: The Protestant Bible in English

1. *Defensor Fidei*, a title still claimed by the British monarch, and the initials F. D. still appear on the British pound.
2. This is how Tyndale was sometimes written in the sixteenth century, though it is not common.
3. His BA was received in 1512 and MA in 1515.
4. This is the central thesis of David Daniell, *William Tyndale: A Biography* (New Haven, CT: Yale University Press, 2001). Any exploration of Tyndale must begin with this biography.
5. *Treacle* is similar to *molasses* in North American usage.
6. Cf. Gerald Bray, *Translating the Bible: From William Tyndale to King James* (London: Latimer Trust, 2010).

Chapter 11: The King James Bible

1. David Roach, "LifeWay Research Finds Americans Still Appreciate KJV," April 21, 2011, Lifeway.com, https://lifewayresearch.com/2011/04/21/lifeway-research-finds-americans-still-appreciate-kjv/.
2. A confessional point subsequently forgotten by the Bishops' Bible under Elizabeth.
3. *Calvinism* is a term that arose long after the Reformation itself. The problem is that Calvin neither created the Reformed faith (the way Luther did Lutheranism) nor was the lone voice in its confessions. In fact, there was already a Reformed faith in Zurich before Calvin converted.
4. Strangely, Knox relied mostly on arguments from natural law and even medieval statues to make the case and only somewhat based his view on the Bible. On Knox, see Jane Dawson, *John Knox* (New Haven: Yale University Press, 2016).
5. He remained king of Scotland, which meant the two nations were now united. However, there had been five previous kings named James *in Scotland*, none *in England*—hence the quirky way some history books record his name as *James VI and I*.
6. The essential narrative is told in Benson Bobrick, *Wide as the Waters: The Story of the English Bible and the Revolution It Inspired* (New York: Simon & Schuster, 2001), 199–266.
7. Covered in David Daniell, *The Bible in English* (New Haven: Yale University Press, 2003), 358–68.
8. This same point is made in Gerald Bray, *Translating the Bible: From William Tyndale to King James* (London: Latimer Trust, 2010).
9. J. I. Mombert, *English Versions of the Bible* (London: Samuel Bagster and

Sons, 1907), 383. Mombert goes on to give several pages of issues in the KJV.

10. The Vulgate got this right, but the KJV made the name Joshua a popular name in English ever since.

Chapter 12: The Modern Bible Movements

1. Jonathan Swift, "A Proposal for Correcting, Improving and Ascertaining the English Tongue," ed. Jack Lynch, Rutgers.com, https://andromeda. rutgers.edu/~jlynch/Texts/proposal.html.
2. A. S. Herbert, *Historical Catalogue of Printed Editions of the English Bible, 1525–1961* (London: British and Foreign Bible Society, 1968), 142–44.
3. Robin Scroggs, "John Wesley as Bible Scholar," *Journal of Bible and Religion* 28.4 (Oct. 1960): 415–22.
4. The Bible is reprinted as Julia E. Smith, *The Holy Bible* (London: Forgotten Books, 2017).
5. Robert Young, *The Holy Bible, Consisting of the Old and New Covenants; Translated according to the Letter and Idioms of the Original Languages*, rev. ed. (Edinburgh: George Adam Young & Co., 1887). Citation is from the preface (unpaginated).
6. He is also remembered for playing an active role in the trial of Anne Hutchinson, who was charged with antinomianism.
7. See Mark Noll, *In the Beginning Was the Word: The Bible in American Public Life, 1492–1783* (Oxford: Oxford University Press, 2015), for background.

Chapter 13: The Bible Today—and Tomorrow

1. Today it is the Naval and Military Bible Society.
2. The story is discussed in David Bebbington, *Evangelicalism in Modern Britain: A History from the 1730s to the 1980s* (Abingdon, UK: Routledge, 2004), 84ff.
3. In 1815, five cents and fifty cents, adjusted for inflation.
4. On this material, the best source is D. Daniell, *The Bible in English* (New Haven, CT: Yale University Press, 2003), 683–700.
5. The total days in session, accounting for breaks: New Testament—407 days; Old Testament—792 days.
6. The RV itself also became known as the *English Revised Version*.
7. Background again in Daniell, *Bible in English*, 734–68. An analysis and critique of the NIV are in Andreas J. Köstenberger and David A. Croteau, *Which Bible Translation Should I Use? A Comparison of Four Major Recent Versions* (Nashville: B&H, 2012), 78–156.
8. Daniel Wallace provides a survey of these translations, with a much more detailed taxonomy of each group and how they relate—as well as comments on their use of the biblical languages; see "Why So Many Versions?," March 19–21, 2001, Bible.org, https://bible.org/ seriespage/4-why-so-many-versions.